BAUDELAIRE

AND THE SYMBOLISTS

From Dessins de Baudelaire, Librairie Gallimard, Paris

JEANNE DUVAL: Drawing by Baudelaire

BAUDELAIRE
AND THE SYMBOLISTS

FIVE ESSAYS

by

PETER QUENNELL

Ce qui fut baptisé: le *Symbolisme,*
se résume très simplement dans l'intention commune à plusieurs familles
de poètes . . . de "reprendre à la
Musique, leur bien." Le secret de ce
mouvement n'est pas autre.

Paul Valéry : Variété

KENNIKAT PRESS
Port Washington, N. Y./London

BAUDELAIRE AND THE SYMBOLISTS

First published in 1929
Reissued in 1970 by Kennikat Press
Library of Congress Catalog Card No: 76-111315
SBN 8046-0935-7

Manufactured by Taylor Publishing Company   Dallas, Texas

ESSAY AND GENERAL LITERATURE INDEX REPRINT SERIES

I am indebted to the editors of *The New Statesman, The Criterion, Life and Letters,* for permission to reprint the substance of various essays and reviews which have appeared in their columns; to the Librairie Gallimard for permission to reproduce Baudelaire's drawing of Jeanne Duval, and to the Musée Carnavalet two drawings, *The Crinoline* and *The Dancer,* by Constantin Guys.

Contents

List of Illustrations

ix

Apology

THE intention of this book is not learned; indeed, supposing I am asked from what quarter or during what intimacy I acquired the presumption requisite for my series of critical portraits, like the younger Dumas when some arrogant lady demanded of him: "and where was it, do tell me, M. Dumas, that you were enabled to study the *femme du monde?*", chez moi, madame! I too should be obliged to answer,—less arrogantly, perhaps, but insinuating that I too prefer that kind of discreet pillow-companionship, that same knowledge of important trifles and momentous personal vagaries, as against the doubtful privilege of accompanying my subjects into the *grand monde* where an assurance greater than mine bends over their thrones, flattering, courting and appraising them. . . . And yet, after all, should my text fail, then, I realise, apologetic commentary must be quite superfluous; or it may still be worth the writing in so far as it can help a reader to distinguish between omissions which are voluntary and omissions which are the product of ignorance or sheer inattention. Describing Baudelaire, for example, a central figure within whose radius I have attempted to group the smaller presences of Gérard de Nerval, Villiers de l'Isle-Adam, Mallarmé and the rest, I have deliberately omitted the mention of Poe's influence and deliberately minimised the effect usually said to have been exercised upon his development by the dogma and phraseology of the Catholic Church; both have been exaggerated. And again, describing Rimbaud and Mallarmé, I have refused the invitation of several critical detours which, although by no means unfruitful, have now been so thoroughly trampled out that, until the dust-clouds subside, they are not likely to afford the traveller a very fresh or inspiriting prospect. Sometimes employing a method of interrogation which is confined to the scrutiny of an author's work, sometimes resorting to the more personal method which deals in letters, recorded statements, unfledged aspirations, unfulfilled plans, I have tried to elicit those fragmentary responses that, granted the essentially incomplete nature of human aesthetic accomplishment and the inadequacy of the modern intelligence by which it is received, are the most satisfying we can expect from the mouthpiece of any literary oracle. The past gives its reply; the critic confusedly expresses it; and, just as the Delphic priesthood lent the chaotic outpourings of their Sibyl a definite rhythmical and poetic form, so the poet of the future must assimilate and recast the fragmentary discoveries of the critic, giving them that consistency, that harmony, that concrete and substantial grace which of himself and unaided the critic can never hope to instil.

CHARLES BAUDELAIRE

How such a poet spent his days, what kind of a man he was, what measure of personal success crowned his life, are questions seldom asked more fruitlessly than when we apply them to the remains of Charles Baudelaire. The records he left behind him are voluminous, detailed, communicative, and yet an air of singular reticence guards his name. He had written much, lived profusely, uttered manifold appeals, complaints, protestations; their burden is so persistent, and, echoing beyond the grave, so reproachful, that, winding themselves round a reader's pity, they may temporarily quite obscure from him the direction upon which he set out. There have been some men, he should remember, who died many years before the sheet was pulled over their faces; some who, because they enjoyed a secondary, superior, though parasitic, form of life, have made their whole existence one long process of dying. Baudelaire, as I shall try to show him, presents the phenomenon of a poet in whose unhappy nature the creative has completely subordinated all the other faculties. Thus, viewed from Baudelaire's standpoint, *Poetic Inspiration* becomes the parasite which, entering by a covert chink, unprotected at first and microscopic, gradually obsesses all the functions of the body. Sensible enough of the advantages of its position, it does not press its captive hard; some freedom it allows him, liberty to haunt his usual walks, time to move house and to move again, to change street for street, quarter for quarter. Still, his servitude is arduous. "Ce que je souffre en vivant", Baudelaire wrote to his mother in 1861, "vois-tu c'est inexprimable." The letter which includes that sentence was written six years before his death; there were another three years in Paris, two years of tedious exile spent in Brussels, a last tragic year of aphasia and idiocy. His incubus had deserted its creature, and now his dereliction was complete. Swift's Irish deanery, the old man wandering back and forth along its rooms and passages, peering with hollow, commiseratory murmur at his own reflection in the glass, making to wrench the living eyeball from the socket, till he had at length relapsed into mere "incessant strains of obscenity and swearing", was a prison hardly more terrible in its degree than the mortuary chamber which enclosed Baudelaire's final period. Part paralysed, he could move his limbs, and, while he did not speak, had the consolation of, like a parrot, swearing and objurgating on a single note: *Cré Nom! Cré Nom!* Eventually he could neither move nor speak, and it was only with a certain difficulty that they taught him to greet his mother and remark on the fineness of a warm and sunny day.

A suppressed malady had found him out; thus we explain his death. But no physiological hypothesis can explain the manner of his life. It is a perspective of which every line recedes towards some consideration affecting his work. A narrow and retreating plane his life exposes, his work a broad and infinitely variegated surface. Even his portraits, the *simulacra* of his outward features drawn by his own or by another hand, reveal the same characteristic. They are uniformly reticent; they betray, all of them, a suspicious self-defensive gleam which defies closer scrutiny. The portrait commonly accounted best gives the scantiest account of what were his actual lineaments. Yet Manet is said to have been captivated by the likeness, and to have refrained deliberately from touching it a second time. Thus, far back amid the tree-boles, among a crowd of personages more assertive, more lively and more speciously elegant, —the painter himself, for instance, well thrust towards the front and fixing you at once with the dominant glitter of his monocle,—Baudelaire's features flit past in a sort of triangular cloud. They are indistinct, but the effect they make against that solid, prosperous-looking encampment of men and women is strangely individual. Their detachment is arresting. The position occupied by Baudelaire's portrait in the group entitled *Concert aux Tuileries* might be taken to symbolise the anomalous place which this poet had occupied in contemporary esteem. Widely known and generally regarded as the author of one or two macabre and licentious pieces, his verse was admired by the best judges, everywhere praised by sensible critics, but with the praise was often mingled a shadow of mistrust, of almost personal resentment.[1] Sainte-Beuve, when Baudelaire at the time of the notorious *procès* invoked his sympathy and help, had defended, it is true, the quality and intentions of *Les Fleurs du Mal*, but lukewarmly, with a threadbare show of critical impartiality that scarcely conceals the unwillingness with which the ageing critic had approached his task. Yet Baudelaire was Sainte-Beuve's "dear child"; to Baudelaire the elder man was "l'oncle Beuve", a well-loved though slightly ridiculous mentor! Small wonder, then, if casual acquaintances were at no pains to swallow down the instinctive distrust and dislike that Baudelaire's personality aroused. A mass of frigid affectations, the Goncourts thought, noticing his exquisitely tended hands, unmuffled neck and closely cropped hair. "Une vraie toilette de guillotiné," they remarked, committing their phrase like a *bibelot* to the shelves

[1] . . . il demeure avéré que cet homme supérieur garda toujours quelque chose d'inquiétant et d'énigmatique, même pour les amis intimes (Bourget, *Essais de Psychologie Contemporaine*). But see also Banville's *Lettres Chimériques* for an expression of the contrary opinion.

4

of an already abounding and overflowing collection. The Goncourts' description recalls several portraits taken about the same period. An earlier portrait, much earlier, displays the lineaments of a young man, still agreeably entangled in all the illusions and aspirations generally considered proper to his age. The poet is bearded; he droops one hand, pillows his cheek upon the fingers of the other:

> Oisive jeunesse
> A tout asservie . . .

He was busy accumulating debts, burning up his little patrimony in a way of life, modest, sumptuous, but pitched a fraction higher than the narrow margins of his personal fortune would allow. Sure enough of his tastes and antipathies, he was still unsure of his direction and, provided the *direction* could be made clear, whether or not he had the strength to pursue it to its end; hence the look of expectancy and fretfulness united. Beside this portrait any of the later photographs are expressive of a dreadful distance traversed. The hair is close-cut, and the lips and chin are shaven like a priest's. Like a priest's, too, is the entire physiognomy, and conscious, I think, of the resemblance, under its straggling circlet of dark hair. The half-smile seems almost lipless, shut as tightly as a heavy box-lid. The corners of the mouth are depressed as if it were by a muscular tension spreading from the upper part of the face. Baudelaire's self-portraits,—for he was an accomplished and, sometimes, a brilliant draughtsman,—accentuate and parody those characteristics, the furtive, monkish air and sidelong glances of those eyes which roll distracted in their context like two imprisoned globes of foreign material. As for the body, it was usually encased in a garment Baudelaire had himself designed to meet the varied requirements of working and living: his *frac*, dark, formal, yet capacious and easy, not unlike a monastic habit. Later, again, he grew his hair, and it was thus he walked abroad with Constantin Guys—then an elderly man, as, indeed, though prematurely, was Baudelaire himself—side by side through the purgatorial region of gas-lit restaurants and dancing-places both of them loved to observe, greyish locks tumbling forth abundantly from beneath a wide-brimmed *haut de forme*, his throat heavily swaddled in the episcopalian violet of an old silk scarf.

One further particularity must be added and the rough outline I have proposed will be fairly comprehensive;—it is the look of extreme and painful mobility, not obscured but, unawares, displayed by the stony corrugation of the facial muscles. "While I was but young," Baudelaire confessed to his mother, "*étant très jeune*, I contracted a syphilitic infection."

It was a determining factor in his unhappiness, yet far less serious, I suppose, than the admission contained in a letter he wrote immediately after leaving school. "I am worse off now", he declared, "than ever I was at school. At school I occupied myself little enough with my work; still, occupy myself I did. When I was expelled, that shook me up . . . but nowadays *nothing, nothing*. It is not enjoyable, not poetic indolence, but a stupid, splenetic laziness —*indolence maussade et niaise*. . . . Of the spirit of activity which tilted me, sometimes towards good, sometimes towards evil, remains absolutely nothing, only laziness, ill-humour, tedium."

He had noticed, in brief, the earliest symptoms of that mysterious disease of the will, "l'acedia, maladie des moines", mentioned by subsequent diagnoses of his own character with increasing bitterness in proportion as it seemed the more effectually to counteract every plan of possible escape into an outer world of material well-being and assured spiritual tranquillity. Already he must have known the extremes of despair which, for a sufferer from that malady, are combined of a sense of absolute inertia, a sense of nightmare powerlessness, and of the poignant irrealisable desire towards activity and movement. Could he but lift his hand, runs the sleeper's inward persuasion, and lift it but so far as to brush his flank or side, this single gesture would be enough to dislodge

the oppression weighing on his breast and eyelids; in
a single sharp, triumphant effort, it would lay bare
the ponderously sealed-up founts of waking energy;
they would dispatch their forces, at first hesitant and
intermittent, but presently with a doubled and re-
doubled vehemence, like a flood of waters bubbling
down the shallow irrigation-channels of some
parched and exhausted garden; he would stir, con-
vulsively and then with deliberate purpose, raise his
eyelids and wake. In a ghastly pantomime, the sleeper
dreams that he has woken, and dreams that he has
moved his hand, time and time again, before he can, in
fact, summon up sufficient strength to perform either
miracle. Miraculous it appears, since he seems to venture into a state of blessedness attainable solely by an
inhuman exercise of faith. Supine and rigid, he wakes
and sleeps together, but neither takes comfort in the
oblivion of sleep nor enjoys the full freedom of his
waking hours. And so, for the victim of acedia, the
twin states of activity and inactivity are as one, and,
though convicted in his own eyes of the deepest
sloth, his mind is none the less ceaselessly occupied,
if it is only with the impossibility of making any
movement. Results the continuous inner turmoil,
whose traces I have pretended to detect in Baudelaire's portrait, and, the tension snapping, a cry of
sudden alarm: "Je me dis avec une sorte de terreur;
l'important est de prendre l'habitude du travail et de

faire de ce désagréable compagnon mon unique jouissance. Car il viendra un temps où je n'en aurai plus d'autre." It shall be daily work, undertaken with merciless regularity, morning after morning; better work badly, he reflects elsewhere, than not work at all. Work, then! he determines, like a sleeper who relies upon the occult power of a simple gesture of the hand which shall free him from his intolerable load. The poet, too, sketches across the void a phantasmal anticipatory movement, some project of action, a fervent, lucid dream, but which incontinently dissolves, leaving behind it, as it evaporates, a freezing sense of inertia. It is not the effort of work he fears, or so he tells himself;—it is an insuperable disgust of its products. The futility of literature, whispered in his ear low and insidious:

> Alors, j'ai fait d'la littérature,
> Mais le Démon de la Vérité
> Sifflotait tout l'temps à mes côtés:
> "Pauvre! as-tu fini tes écritures" . . .

—swells at last to certitude, and he reaches that condition of absolute spiritual paralysis described so feelingly by the *English Opium-Eater*—with whom, as well as in superficial traits, Baudelaire had several essential points in common. His table, De Quincey wrote, was heaped with half-realised projects, but a kind of nausea always drove him back. No, it was unconquerable, that aversion! And, like De Quincey, day by day and whole weeks and months on end, Baudelaire would watch the testimony of the outside world pile up against him, unopened letters recalling unpaid bills or claiming unwritten articles, mixed with dejected dusty swags of uncorrected galley-proof.

Acedia is a disease which haunts the dismal cells and comfortless ambulatories and refectories of great monastic institutions. It is the bane of mystics, interrupting in a deadly rhythm the life of contemplation, prayers and praise. Incidentally, then, as a modern French critic has pointed out, Baudelaire attests a latent power of concentration when he arraigns his own impotence. But what issue from his trouble can he expect? A mystic embraces the fixity of God's image; a monk obeys the rule of his Order. Naturally impatient of control, Baudelaire could accept no regimen which was not of his own making, did not precisely answer the exigences of his own case. Besides, there is the will to unhappiness, for Baudelaire very strong, deriving its impetus from the remote past. During the first and most impressionable period of childhood, he had been the inhabitant of one of those Edens, chance-formed, when a father drops off and leaves his child in the secure and possessive enjoyment of its mother. The paternal obstacle removed, it can surround its beloved with a wealth of fondness, made up equally of the spontaneous gifts of affection and of continuous demands upon her interest and time; it need fear the irruption of no lover, stronger and more masterful than itself; its native sensuality springs up very fierce and, since its progress is unhampered, exceptionally pure. Baudelaire's father had died when he was six years old. Thenceforward Madame Baudelaire was his entirely to engross. She was young, charming, a fount of voluptuous associations:

Le goût précoce des femmes (he notes in *Fusées*). Je confondais l'odeur de la fourrure avec l'odeur de la femme. Je me souviens. . . . Enfin, j'aimais ma mère pour son élégance. J'étais donc un dandy précoce.

Their perfect amity was completed by the presence of Mariette, Madame Baudelaire's servant, a country-woman, as substantial and rough a spirit as her mistress was *sensible* and fine-drawn, and, in Baudelaire's devotion, her foil and complement. Mariette's name preserved for him a sort of talismanic value; she is the "servante au grande cœur" of *Tableaux Parisiens*, a *revenant* whose voiceless assiduity put him to acute remorse:

Lorsque la bûche siffle et chante, si le soir,
Calme, dans le fauteuil je la voyais s'asseoir,
Si, par une nuit bleue et froide de décembre,
Je la trouvais tapie en un coin de ma chambre,
Grave, et venant du fond de son lit éternel
Couver l'enfant grandi de son œil maternel,
Que pourrais-je répondre à cette âme pieuse . . .?

11

The short spell of amorous calm under whose dispensation they lived, and how intense it was and how precious in recollection after thirty and more years, is the material of another poem, to which I shall have occasion to refer later. *Then* he had been happy, Baudelaire cried, expressly confining his happiness, at forty years old, to that brief luminous interlude. But it had lasted scarcely two years. François Baudelaire had died during the February of 1827; in the November of 1828 his widow married again. Her son was distraught, wrung by the extraordinary violence of childish jealousy. Madame Baudelaire's passion for her second husband could not be disguised, and the contemplation of it aggravated his smart, till it seemed that he could never forgive the initial injury done him and that his hurt was beyond all cure. Cruelty, though, afforded a certain temporary assuagement; Madame Baudelaire's lover became the tormentor of Madame Aupick. He attacked her through the medium of her husband, but the General's fibre was too coarse and his disciplinary methods too drastic to afford a very satisfactory medium for the impetuous overflow of loverly hatred. She would be more effectually punished, Baudelaire thought, in the spectacle of her son's misery.

So, suffering was a habit of mind, even a necessity, a stimulus to which he grew accustomed. Happiness

was to be understood either as connoting the un-
believable, irrecapturable tranquillity of that "green
paradise of infantine loves" which flourished between the sixth and eighth years of his age:

> Je n'ai pas oublié, voisine de la ville,
> Notre blanche maison, petite mais tranquille;
> Sa Pomone de plâtre et sa vieille Vénus
> Dans un bosquet chétif cachant leurs membres nus,
> Et le soleil, le soir, ruisselant et superbe,
> Qui, derrière la vitre où se brisait sa gerbe,
> Semblait, grand œil ouvert dans le ciel curieux,
> Contempler nos dîners longs et silencieux,
> Répandant largement ses beaux reflets de cierge
> Sur la nappe frugale et les rideaux de serge:

—a recollection all the more cherished because, seen
in retrospect, so insecure, hoisted like a halcyon's
raft among breaking wave-crests and flying drops of
salt,—or else that graver, adult mood, perhaps hardly
deserving the name, which follows after unhappiness
and takes its place as a vibrant hush follows the
quivering strokes of a bell. Happiness was a relief
from distress, but pervaded by the reverberation of
its opposite; for Baudelaire no mean was practicable,
and, writing or speaking of his work, it is important
that the disability should be remembered: that we
should insist that here a man had been born, quite
incapable of normal satisfactions, of the normal facile
balance of small pains and smaller compensatory
pleasures; that, had he willed it even, he would have

proved himself lacking in the bastard ingenuity which has enabled countless smaller writers to soften the acerbities of life with the borrowed amenities of art. Integrally a portion of his art, Baudelaire could no more separate himself, so far as to exploit in it a source of objective complacency, than the splendid animal can take a prolonged dispassionate delight in testing the fineness of its muscles or in the rapt admiration of a striped or marbled skin.

*　　　*　　　*

It is a condition of the poet's life,—and symptomatic, I suppose, of the footing of almost complete subordination to his art upon which a true poet exists,—that every personal problem which engages him should be metamorphosed and ultimately reappear as a problem of aesthetics. Such solutions the goddesses of poetry favour, when merely human ingenuity has thrust the problem away: were it not for its essential difficulty, the set of figures it concerns is presented under far too embroiled and slovenly a guise! Insoluble, then, in terms of life, Baudelaire's multiple perplexities, translated into terms of art, received a solution I shall attempt to follow through the preliminary calculations included in the volume of his journals and in certain pages of his critical essays. Direct indebtedness there is little; yet, besides an influence which, though making itself felt comparatively late, was of a profound and lasting effect, I must also mention the influence of his father. François Baudelaire, we know, had died while his son was six years old, but his example—partly from a memory of the sympathetic relation which had subsisted between them and partly from the spirit of sheer contrariety inhabiting the younger man, a natural recoil towards the memory of an indulgent father from the oppressive reality of a despised and resented step-parent—Charles elected to emulate, thus first of all entering upon a course in which the development of his tastes and interests gradually confirmed him. François Baudelaire had been an agent and occasional tutor in the family of the ducs de Choiseul-Praslin, and, during this contact, extending over the greater part of his career, an intimate as well as a servitor of the house, he had adopted a manner of thinking and behaving foreign to his century, particularly foreign to his rank, but of which the agreeable impression upon his son was never afterwards effaced,—the old man driving away street dogs with a tall cane he carried about with him in his promenades, his dilettante relish of the arts, the ceremonious salutations of which he was pro- digal, the protective atmosphere he had created: "*Vieux mobilier Louis XVI, antiques, consulat, pastel, société dix-huitième siècle.*" Fortified by that memory, precociously at his ease among the varied refine-

ments, mannerisms and minor sensuous gratifica-
tions which had endeared to him his father's mode
of life, Baudelaire was—he has made the assertion
himself, in words which can leave no doubt at all of
the degree of emphasis which he thought it deserved
—a dandy from his mother's lap: a dandy *of* his
mother's lap, indeed, his dandyism warmed and nur-
tured there, since it was from her presence he derived
his first and keenest sensations of voluptuous pleasure; about her person, too, that his mysticism first
wrapped its web; in her treachery that his first and
bitterest suffering had originated.

Above all, he enjoyed her elegance:—"J'étais
donc un dandy précoce". Dandyism, much vulgarised word, as it was employed by Baudelaire and as
every commentator of his work is obliged to resort
to it, should be understood as connoting the attitude
of a poet towards his surroundings of space and time
at its severest, least frivolous, most vigilant and exacting. The superficial aspect of his dandyism, his
appreciation of fine sober apparel and the elaborate
courtesy of his manners, was inherited, we know,
from the memory of François Baudelaire. But the
primary influence which I have cited was, I believe,
the example of Constantin Guys. In Guys, Baudelaire had recognised, or thought that he had recognised, an embodiment of the artist's functions carried
to a pitch of almost complete selflessness and entire

impersonality. Guys was an arduous workman, but he was also so acute a critic of his own efforts that he tore up the good half of what he produced. Rigorously self-critical, while he worked it was with an ardour so extravagant that it kept him bent over his table until the dawn; and, not sparing the necessary pause to find a rag or scrap of paper, he would wipe his reeking pen across the open front of his shirt. As smaller artists have fostered a name, Guys cherished his anonymity; it would have cost him genuine distress if he had seen his name published, and, in his magnificent essay *Le Peintre de la Vie Moderne*, Baudelaire was obliged to shelter the draughtsman's identity under a single letter, designating him *tout court* Monsieur G. Appropriately enough, his eulogy of Constantin Guys is also his chief eulogy of dandyism; it contains a passage which, besides setting the tenor of this stringent discipline he hoped to establish amid the apparent disorder and aimless profusion of his life, may provide an incidental hint for the consideration of certain larger questions which a study of his dogma is likely to provoke.

"Le mal se fait sans effort, *naturellement*," he wrote in his *Éloge de Maquillage*, one of the thirteen chapters or subsections into which *Le Peintre de la Vie Moderne* is divided, ". . . le bien est toujours le produit d'un *art*. Tout ce que je dis de la nature

comme mauvaise conseillère en matière de morale
. . . peut être transporté dans l'ordre du beau." He
insists upon the homogeneity of his beliefs, aesthetic
and moral, and describes the main principle informing them. Virtue or beauty, he declares, thus once
and for all wrenching himself free from the over-
lordship of eighteenth-century *philosophes* and nineteenth-century Romantics, is a highly *artificial* product and can only be maintained with difficulty, by
deliberate and unresting effort against the constant
jealous pressure of natural forces. Than the cultivation of Simplicity, he adds, nothing more depraved,
a work of art excelling just in so far as it has separated
itself from and shows smaller and smaller trace of the
raw material in which it germinated. We attain to
virtue, runs his parallel proposition, not by removing the incrusted deposits of evil and so, at bottom,
discovering the fictitious innocence and happiness of
primaeval man, but during a long process of manu-
facture, of actual adornment you might say, trans-
muting and overlaying our natural criminality or
indifference with as indefatigable a skill as some great
courtesan would spend upon the sallow texture of
her morning cheeks. For it was a *Défense of Fard*
Baudelaire was writing when he stumbled across
this definition of his *credo*, and again and again, we
shall find, the associations of the dressing-table and
the mirror are, in Baudelaire's philosophy, thus

18

closely connected to the highest considerations of art and life—the Dandy's meticulous labour beneath his glass immediately recalling the labours of a great artist, equally intense, equally fervid in its care of "minute particulars". He notes the fundamental disinterestedness of such strivings after perfection, and sees evinced in them the nobility of a creature which, though still deeply sunk in the animalism of its natural state, is always ready to assume fresh burdens, new and thankless tasks. "Je suis ainsi conduit à regarder la parure", he remarks, "comme un des signes de la noblesse primitive de l'âme humaine."

Elsewhere, in a sentence not less significant, he applauds "la majesté superlative des formes artificielles". It was their artificiality charmed him, the beauty of the fulfilled purpose, the dignity of a complete design, projected into the world as full of strength and delicacy as, at its birth, it had been weak and helpless. These preoccupations shaped the character of his verse; and, thus, his preferred imagery, startling sometimes and occasionally harsh in its effect, is of intention sober and ineffusive almost to the point of seeming too finely strained. The pedantic beauty of great sailing-ships, moored alongside the quay, — each the monstrous edifice of patience and knowledge, every shroud and spar tightly threaded against some known, calculated danger, quiescent, yet, while it rocks its yards across the sun, each apparently meditating an immediate, urgent flight,—made frequent and profound inroads on his sensibility. "La beauté sobre et élégante du navire moderne", he wrote and, in the *Journaux Intimes*, a citation, perhaps, than which there are few more important for the just understanding of his work:

I imagine that the infinite and mysterious charm which exists in the contemplation of a ship, the contemplation especially of a ship under way, is derived in the first place from its regularity and symmetry, which, in the same degree as complication and harmony, are among the primordial requirements of the human spirit; and, in the second place, from the successive multiplication and generation of all those curves and visionary figures described through space by the solid elements of which it is composed.

The poetic idea, liberated by this operation of linear movement, consists in the hypothesis of a being vast, immeasurably complicated, none the less eurhythmic, a creature abounding in genius, suffering and sighing with all the sighs, all the aspiration of the human kind.

Infinite and mysterious charm, rising, you notice, from the contemplation of an object definite and perfectly concrete, of an equipage so precisely and sparsely designed that the perspectives surrounding it are a thousand times increased. What more adequate symbol of his own improved poetic method, more satisfactory expression of his dandyism?

Notre âme est un trois-mâts, cherchant son Icarie.

. . . But it would be superfluous here to reassemble the large number of other references of a kindred sort, though elsewhere it may be convenient to deal with them one by one, the ship depending for its place in Baudelaire's imagery not so much on its association with the sea—"spectacle . . . infiniment et éternellement agréable"—as on his conception of it as a being, intricate, immense, exquisitely symmetrical, possessed of a regular oscillatory motion, just such a fascination as the undulatory progress of a woman's skirt: above all, *symmetrical*, like the lustre which dangles in the theatre ceiling,—"lumineux, cristallin, compliqué, circulaire et symétrique", —towards which he had always raised his eyes, Baudelaire declared in a paragraph of *Mon Cœur Mis à Nu*, with delight and awe, a prick of pleasurable wonder recurrent ever since he was a child.

It is impressions such as these,—the rumour of a woman's skirts, evocative of a maternal tenderness, a swimming haze of lights that may, perhaps, recall our earliest adventure into the realms of scenic illusion, —that interbreed and multiply, and are the prime factors to which any poetic style, even the most complicated and allusive, can ultimately be reduced. And more important still than these impressions, momentous as they are in the history of our poetic development, is the sensibility delicate enough to receive them, retentive enough of its treasure to hand it down, unfaded and undiminished, through a long, disorderly procession of years. The impressions of childhood are, generally, less indistinct than those of maturity, because childhood is defenceless, could not if it would make headway against the crushing impact of disappointment, is, literally, *overcome* by an access of pleasurable emotion, employs a livelier, more barbaric fetichism in its painted travesty of the outside world. Age, accumulating and elaborating defences, learns the knack of safeguarding its calm, and, since every keen emotion is a potential threat, makes a constant and unscrupulous use of it, upon smaller and smaller provocation. How, without unhealthily retarding his growth, he can preserve something of this ingenuous clarity which, in the past, has enabled him to see men as trees walking, is a dilemma which confronts every artist. It is typical of Baudelaire that the solution he proposed should be so unsparingly thorough, that as far as he applied it to his own case he should have shown himself so indecisive and vacillating, and that, finally, it should have been by devious and involuntary paths he reached a point which he had long despaired of ever gaining by a simple exercise of will. Meanwhile, there are contradictions. . . . One should keep oneself perfectly open, he said . . . and, at another time, that one must establish a rule, found an order and submit one's life to a regular discipline, marked off by the hours of the day and by the days of the calendar: "*Toilette, prière, travail*", work itself subdivided,—days put aside for settling arrears of correspondence, days for the sorting of old manuscripts and letters, days for the classification of his prints and drawings. One must work daily: "L'inspiration", he announces, "est décidément la sœur du travail journalier", yet later admits that it is idleness and continued leisure which has proved the chief nursery of his talent: "C'est par le loisir que j'ai, en partie, grandi." At all events, the proposed classification, docketing, index-making, once attempted, proves quite beyond his power, and, though lamenting the confusion, he is content to let it stay as it is, heaping up under his eyes as a perpetual reproach, gathering its thick blackish pall of dust and regrets:

> J'ai plus de souvenirs que si j'avais mille ans.
>
> Un gros meuble à tiroirs encombré de bilans,
> De vers, de billets doux, de procès, de romances,
> Avec de lourds cheveux roulés dans des quittances,
> Cache moins de secrets que mon triste cerveau.
> C'est une pyramide, un immense caveau,
> Qui contient plus de morts que la fosse commune . . .

The sheer mass of material is beyond his energy to raise. And so, efforts of will avail him nothing; the proposed escape was, after all, a brief circular detour which has brought him back to the condition of things he had meant to leave behind him for ever; it may bring us back again to the juncture from which we originally set out—Baudelaire's aesthetic scheme, that is to say, as it is exemplified in his study of Constantin Guys.

Returning to his examination of the draughtsman, a figure with whom the poet and critic, we feel, is identifying his own existence more and more nearly: "Consider this man", he exclaims, "as being a man-child,—*prenez-le . . . pour un homme-enfant*, for a man possessing at every moment of the day the genius of childhood, a man, in short, for whom familiarity has robbed of its brilliance no single aspect of our common life." "Le génie de l'enfance" he has previously described in the following passage: "For the child everything is *new*; he is always *intoxicated*. Nothing bears a more striking resemblance to what is called inspiration than the joy with which forms and colours are absorbed by the child" . . . lines which confirm that remarkable account of the vividness of childish sensation given by an English metaphysical poet:

The corn was orient and immortal wheat, which never should be reaped, nor was ever sown. I thought it had stood from everlasting to everlasting. . . . The gates were at first the end of the world. The green trees when I saw them first through one of the gates transported and ravished me; their sweetness and unusual beauty made my heart to leap, and almost mad with ecstasy, they were such strange and wonderful things. The Men! O what venerable and reverend creatures did the aged seem! Immortal Cherubims! And young men glittering and sparkling Angels, and maids strange seraphic pieces of life and beauty! Boys and girls tumbling in the street, and playing, were moving jewels. I knew not that they were born or should die; but all things abided eternally as they were in their proper places.

Noticing, like Traherne, the kind of nervous shock, of partial derangement, which often accompanies these precocious manifestations of sensibility, "J'oserai pousser plus loin", Baudelaire continues, "j'affirme que l'inspiration a quelque rapport avec la *congestion*, et que toute pensée sublime est accompagnée d'une secousse nerveuse, plus ou moins forte, qui retentit jusque dans le cervelet." Then, realising, no doubt, that his profuse employment of analogies, drawn from the state of childhood, might seem, on the face of it, to conflict with standards of artificiality as rigorous as those he has just proclaimed, he goes on to stress the stability of the great artist's nervous organisation compared to the essential instability of the *naïf* or the child: "The man of genius has stable nerves, the child unstable; in the constitution of the one, reason has assumed a preponderant place, while in the constitution of the other, sensibility holds still an almost undisputed sway. Yet genius is, after all, no more than *childhood recaptured* at will, childhood endowed, that it may the better express itself, with an adult organism, a spirit of analysis which will enable it to set in some order the copious mass of material which it has unwittingly acquired"...meantime referring us to a different image which he has outlined somewhat further back in his disquisition —of the artist as a convalescent, the *perpetual convalescent*, he said, a man who, while the rug, reminder of pain and illness, still sags heavily across his knees, looks forth from his window in an irradiation of "profound and mirthful curiosity". For all those who have enjoyed in such merely negative relief a happiness far deeper and more solid than could afford any delight positive and purposeful, this new and curious analogy need scarcely be expanded. They will remember how, during their absence from it, the entire universe seemed to have acquired a novel salience and distinction. Like a landscape after rain, some features of the universe they regarded had rushed forward into brilliant prominence, leaving behind them immensely enlarged perspectives, a sense of almost terrifying propinquity being combined with a sense of unfathomable distance,— mountains, river-beds and distant pastures very near and yet, at the same time, inexpressibly far away, and the whole so intimate, so beautifully co-ordinated that, while you admired the vastness of the arena into which you were peering, you were conscious at the same time of a mastery over it as complete as if it were your own garden you were contemplating, your own plot of ground and water ingeniously designed by yourself, and you were inclined to stretch out your hand and try whether you could not dam up the torrent with a thumb, or with the reverse side of your palm brush away a forest and leave the mountain-slopes clean;—it clung there like a feather-coat of mildew, a dark stain spoiling the whiteness and hardness of the natural rock.

Thus the convalescent, and thus "the perpetual convalescent" or artist,—a child reborn with adult nerves and intelligence,—enjoys an illusion of power over the spectacle he contemplates, power attained by virtue of the inappeasable curiosity which controls him. By the possession of this appetite, Baudelaire concludes, he is immediately to be distinguished from the herd of artists, better called mechanics, whose intelligence is of a merely executive order: "Sauf deux ou trois exceptions . . . la plupart des artistes sont, il faut bien le dire, des brutes très-adroites, de purs manœuvres, des intelligences de village, des cervelles de hameau". A true artist, on the contrary, approximates to the perfect type of dandyism,—"*Homme du monde*, c'est-à-dire homme du monde entier, homme qui comprend le monde et les raisons mystérieuses et légitimes de tous ses usages",—a type which should not imply any notions of satiety, since, though prematurely sophisticated, it is never, in the deadliest meaning of the word, *blasé*, never disillusioned; its capacity for assimilating fresh material persists until the very end.

It may be objected here, that the *Dandy*, the sum total, that is to say, of Baudelaire's numerous reflections upon dandyism, scattered through the pages of his journals and the volumes of his critical essays, is a creature quite beyond the pale of ordinary human life, and certainly very much dissimilar,—as being too heroic, too impassive, too compact of supernatural fortitude,—from the personality of the writer himself. We can reply that, properly, such ideal creations *must* be irrealisable; that, thence, they get the elasticity which enables them to grow as we grow, shrink as we shrink, the continuance of any religious system, for example, depending in large part upon the essential impracticability of the type it proposes. Chimerical then, or neighbouring the class of events which grammarians had in mind when they provided us with a conditional clause expressly designed to cover things "possible but not probable", no single feature of the Dandy's entire composition but might be related to some important and individual feature of its author's own existence. Like Frankenstein's monster, his Dandy ranges Baudelaire's life, of fatal effect as often as it touches the conduct of his personal career,—*there* urging him to the maddest

extravagances, steeling his natural intransigeance,—
none the less a presiding genius of his work, coun-
selling a labour meticulous, scrupulously exact, a
cultivation of those "minute particulars", those *minu-
tiae* of form in which, according to Blake's view of
the nature of a poet's functions, the whole of beauty
must be thought to consist. A bifrontal monster!—
and how ambiguously it glanced both ways at once
may be evinced by a further examination of the
analogy mentioned above. Convalescence implies
previous illness, and perpetual convalescence a perpetual sequence of illness and recovery, an agitation
perpetually maintained, a graph always climbing and
subsiding, and a state of mental and physical health
which allows of no steady interval pitched between
the heights and the depths. At this juncture, I recall a
jotting, committed among other jottings haphazard to
the pages of his notebook, which has long been the
cause of offence to his critics, but which, in their different ways, each of them has considered illuminating
and momentous: "J'ai cultivé mon hystérie", he wrote
in *Mon Cœur Mis à Nu*, "avec jouissance et terreur".
It is obvious, at least, is it not, that an imperious and
very active member of the swarming commonwealth
of interests and desires, which we agree to call a
man, was as determinedly the foe of his quietude as
other and more ineffectual members of the synod
were its persuasive advocates? Admit the perversity

which "chid his fortune from him"; let us also admit, besides the faction merely malcontent, a *reasoned* opposition, serenely resolved that his best hope of poetic victory lay in never stabilising his forces; that his natural mobility should be maintained even at the entire expense of personal happiness and moral calm. For many of our grossest errors, when we scrutinise an artist's work, are directly consequent upon the assumption that it is with a single man we are engaged, and not with a disorderly commonwealth of which now one mob of partisans has the control and now a second, neither fully cognisant of the other's plans and intentions. One voice then, we need not be surprised to learn, lamented the confusion of Baudelaire's life, while, elsewhere, in subdued muttering conclave: 'So it must remain, however ignominious and unpleasant', decided an alien group. Alas, that the inward consciousness of a splendid destiny is so flimsy a thing, that it can hardly compensate its possessor for the smallest material rub: "Que pense la toile sur laquelle on est en train de peindre un chef-d'œuvre? 'On me salit. On me brutalise. On me cache'." . . . But now change the image slightly, and enquire of the fine magnetic needle, pivoted on its eternal centre, what it broods travelling slowly back and forth, what black mood of self-pity and self-abhorrence attends its shuddering oscillation to and fro. "Such irresolution!" no doubt, "a weakness and lack of stability beyond all words to condemn!" in the disgust of its own hypersensitive divagations, quite ignoring the firm pivot upon which it is rooted: "A moment ago I had resolved to point—thus . . . and but an instant later I am under the necessity of a new trembling, painful readjustment",—meanwhile envying the comparative fixity, the admirable show of moral determination made by a nail rusting raggedly in the brickwork of the wall!

*　　*　　*

To appreciate any design, we must be prepared to acknowledge the large element of sheer luck or happy mischance which has entered into its composition. We must also, I think, postulate for each several artist his own particular *daemon* or, in the older sense of the word, *genius*, which, inhabiting the recesses of his person and working its way as covertly and as unconsciously as the digestive system secretes its fluids, is able to nourish and form his mind out of what broken viands the goddess Hazard may care to throw across his path. Then, viewed superficially, every separate stage in his progress may seem to have been conditioned by accident. Examined a little more closely, it will appear that the various requirements of the different stations in the artist's life-history attract, all of them, an appropriate set of circumstances. It is true, maybe, that we can beckon experience; but we cannot determine the strength or velocity with which it will arrive. Hence, the share, and perhaps the only share, that Hazard can take in the arrangement of the artist's life. We are like swimmers, toiling inshore among the surf and now braced to receive the impact of a billow, which, as it happens, goes sweeping harmlessly past them; now lax and unprepared, rolled over by a sudden onset of the waves. Is it presumptuous that we should assume this, at any rate partial, control of the swelling, subsiding storm-ridges of irresistible cause and effect? Certainly, when you consider their respective magnitude, it is more reasonable to conceive of a General Aupick as being drawn out of his course by the exigences of a Baudelaire, as being thrust willy-nilly into Caroline's bed, than to suppose that, once having reached that position, his imminence could cause the smallest deviation in his step-son's devoted path. Yet thus, as far as the Muse of History can distinguish, General Aupick did. But it is important to remember that the detour may have existed before the obstacle.

In adoration of the kind Baudelaire had vowed to his mother, disappointment is implicit; lurking, it waits its opportunity. The opportunity is trifling, the agent of little account. Necessary it is, said the Prophet, that I should be betrayed; yet woe to him

through whom I am betrayed . . . that paradox
hoary with wonder and alarm! Woe to General
Aupick! Flinging away from the memory of a faith-
less love, his future mistresses, the young man decided, should belong to a category which would de-
prive them of the same power to hurt, the same
terrible hold upon the life of his emotions. Instead
of love as he had first experienced it, his frustrate
love for Caroline, he would enthrone the embodiment of sensual habit. Here, again, the personifica-
tion of his need was ready and close at hand. "There
are but two classes of women feasible," he wrote in
his *Conseils aux Jeunes Littérateurs*, "thoroughly
stupid women or trulls—les filles ou les femmes
bêtes, l'amour ou le pot-au-feu—fornication or the
stew-pot." For ever afterwards, he had made up his
mind, he must avoid the exactions, the exhausting
sensiblerie, the eventual treachery of Caroline and
her sort. Jeanne Duval, a mulatress, kept-woman
par excellence, and, his latest biographer has con-
jectured, the realisation of sensual dreams already
formed during his stay in a tropical French colony,
—where Baudelaire had watched a negress scourged
in the market-place, the supple rods falling regularly
across a lean, magnificent back,—had been gathered
up by the poet out of the wings of a small French
theatre and immediately installed by him in a place
in his life from which, henceforward, she was never

entirely dislodged. After their association had lasted quite fourteen years, and at a time when he believed that it was over and done with for good, he could turn to Caroline, always his best comforter it appears (though, poor woman, besides the unfailing tenderness she allowed him, she was also continually giving proof, as his letters informed her, of the most startling insensitiveness and lack of comprehension), and canvass her sympathy for Jeanne, then grown old and no longer seductive, in the following impassioned terms: "My affair with Jeanne," he told her, "an affair of fourteen years' length, is broken off. I did everything that was humanly possible to prevent the rupture. This tearing apart of ourselves, this struggle, lasted full fifteen days. Jeanne persisted in answering me that I had an intolerable nature, and that, anyhow, one day I should thank myself for having taken this step. So much for women's vulgar good-sense. But, on my side, I know that whatever happy chance befalls me, pleasure, affluence or self-esteem, I shall never cease to regret her. Lest you should think that my distress, which, I dare say, you do not understand, is merely childish, I must admit that it is upon her that, like a gambler, I have staked all my hopes; this woman was my sole distraction, she was my one pleasure, my only friend, and, in spite of all the nervous storms of a distracted love-affair, I have never clearly formulated in my mind the idea of an irreparable break. And even now,—perfectly calm as I am,—I surprise myself thinking as often as I see some beautiful object, a fair landscape, no matter what so long as it is charming: 'Why is she not here with me, to admire it, to buy it?' You notice, that I do not hide my sores . . ."

Meanwhile, the quill pen which, upon another occasion, had rendered such a lively, incisive and almost brutally satirical account of his own features, emphasising, as I have said, all that was furtive about them, the eye's *louche* sidelong blink and determined misery of the lipless mouth's downdrawn corners, had also busied itself about Jeanne; and from Jeanne's physiognomy, too, had extracted not so much a likeness, though a brilliant likeness it evidently is, as a panegyric of her vices, a chart of moral defectuosities boldly and unpityingly scored. Thrice, at least, he had portrayed her, and, each time, stressed the hardness and impudence of her gaze; he drew his pen affectionately along the curves of her lean ribs and flanks,—he loved thinness, he said, because it was more indecent than any plump body,—exaggerating the insolent projection of small, sharp-nippled breasts, which strained so greedily against their tight dark covering and got an added relief from the leather strap, with its enormous square of cruel-looking steel buckle, belted in fiercely just beneath them. Her skin was dusky, yellow rather than brown, her nose only slightly flattened, the grain of the skin, betwixt the nostril and the left cheek, marked by a large fleck. A tangle of bows and ribbons crowned her head, and, behind, the masses of her black hair tumbled towards the shoulder-blades rolled up in the swinging meshes of a big, clumsy net. *"Quaerens quem devoret"*, he wrote across the bottom of the paper, and bade us appreciate this phantom as the direct antithesis of himself. Here was a temperament as assertively and unashamedly thrust into the world as his own personality was shamefaced and withdrawn. It was plain enough that, of the two partners of this unequal and unholy alliance, one would suffer most; that, like every pair of lovers, they would alternate the rôles of tormentor and victim, but that the disparity of their mutual sufferings would be more strongly pronounced than, perhaps, is usual. Jeanne could hardly have failed to become aware that her function—and with a detachment, with a kind of intellectual frigidity, an impersonality, in short, above all else calculated to enrage a woman of her breed—was being abused. Rather than enjoy her naïve animalism for its own sake, Baudelaire had made it a weapon which he employed *against* himself. She was involved in the moves of a game, mysterious to her comprehension and utterly distasteful to the primitive yet rigid codes of morality generally professed by her sisterhood. Is it excessive to suppose that the feminine "vulgar good-sense," which she possessed in so high a degree, and, worse still, the characteristic, unexpected *pudeur* upon which her whole life stood based, was profoundly, genuinely outraged? She found a thousand means of revenge, was prolific of a thousand sleights. She destroyed, broke into, pilfered and was assiduous in tearing to pieces the illusion of domestic comfort which, besides the perverse stimulus he derived, Baudelaire had especially hoped for from the years of long and ardent concubinage spent in common. She betrayed him with his barber, he said, and tried no effort at concealment. She drove away his cat, he added bitterly, because he loved cats; because he hated dogs and, like Strindberg, they affected him to the point of physical nausea, she pretended to console his loss by introducing a dog.

It is in this deliberate violence done himself, this assault upon his own moral fastidiousness, that, for a student of his work as apart from the curious amateur of life, lies the importance and inward content of their prolonged *liaison*. Baudelaire, we remember, in that early letter addressed to Caroline, had bewailed the "spirit of activity", now tilting him towards good, now towards evil; can he ever recapture it again? Similarly, during the entire course of his life, no catastrophe, we shall find, does he dread more than a creeping paralysis of his moral functions which should finally obliterate the "two simultaneous postulates, one towards God, the other towards Satan", which (he had declared) are the inseparable companions of a man's every thought. And hence it comes about that the *Question of Evil* takes a larger and larger place in his mind. But I anticipate; at the present stage Baudelaire was still content to revivify his deadened moral sensibilities by, as radically as possible, flouting and damaging them. Thus we shall explain his many perverse and bitter utterances upon Love. Seated amid a company, the theme of whose discussion was Love and wherein reposed its greatest satisfaction, he heard some speakers (he notes in *Fusées*) emit a belief that Love's chief pleasure was in *receiving*, some that it was in *giving*; some said that it was the pleasure of appeased vanity, some the pleasure of humility . . . till, at length, there came an impudent Utopist who affirmed that the supreme pleasure of Love was in providing the motherland with fresh citizens. "Moi, je dis" (he goes on) "la volupté unique et suprême de l'amour gît dans la certitude de faire le *mal*. Et l'homme et la femme savent, de naissance, que dans le mal se trouve toute volupté." Not only the purport of that declaration, which, when it is related to the history of Jeanne Duval and of his earlier disappointed love, can be allowed to speak for itself,—but the manner of its delivery, too, is, I think, significant. That is the assertion of a man (it would seem at the first glance) whom suffering urges towards some hysterical over-statement or misstatement, projected with unsteady violence into the provocative smooth flow of the conversation. "Je dis" . . . acrid emphasis, palp-ably deriving from the bitter-sweet enjoyment with which an inferior kind of distress singles itself out. But once admit Baudelaire's constant inclination to parody his own features, and his factitious enuncia-tion of the above statement, and of many others, becomes much clearer. Baudelaire was his own first imitator (the least permanent examples of his verse are written *in the manner of*, as well as *by*, Charles Baudelaire), besides being a far better caricaturist of his own attitude and way of life than ever was Durandeau. As against Durandeau's rather hesitant and feeble lithographed plate, *Les Nuits de M. Baudelaire*,—Baudelaire agonising upon his col-lapsed truckle-bed, among the thin, squawling cats which infest his attic-room,—the poet himself, under the influence of haschish it is said, has given us a caricatured portrait of his peculiar Satanic affecta-tion, carried to its furthest extreme. The background is the place Vendôme, curiously blurred and dis-torted, its column wavering up tortuously into the clouds; a brightest point in this murky setting, shines the poet's vengeful, sidelong leer; a heavy scarf is furtively pulled up over his chin, a tall black hat suspiciously pulled down towards a projecting stump of black, palely winking cigar,—a shabby, dandiacal figure, yet as portentous as the comet in the sky;—it rushes across the midnight air in a broad, ragged welt of flame.

"So this", a reader may exclaim, "is Mr. Arthur Symons' 'hermit of the brothel', this is Swinburne's 'strange, sad brother' or frigidly preoccupied amateur of vice!" Yes, it was in Baudelaire himself that these misconceptions originated; and, consequently, while removing the thick incrustation deposited by previous critics, we must beware of emulating those restorers of statuary who are so bent on scraping off an anachronistic layer of paint or whitewash that, incidentally, they remove all traces of the original colour. Again, let us remember Baudelaire's dandyism and the degree of almost heroic intransigeance which his attitude implies. "It is beyond my comprehension", he records in *Mon Cœur Mis à Nu*, "how the pure hand can touch a newspaper without an instinctive movement of revulsion . . . and yet it is with the accompaniment of this disgusting *apéritif* that civilised man is accustomed to break his fast. . . ." Elsewhere, he speaks of the immense wave of nausea to which he is inspired by the sight of placarded advertisements. Such universal nausea, it is true, we may all of us have at some time shared, but there are certainly not many whose disgust, once announced, is thenceforward supported by a spirit of consistent and uncompromising opposition:

> Nous avons . . .
>   Salué l'énorme Bêtise,
>   La Bêtise au front de taureau.

We formally express our abhorrence and are thereafter excessively anxious to come to terms; it is easier so. Yet a mere handful—and among them Baudelaire —are as incapable of compromise as, perhaps, their actual desire for repose, for the love, respect, mutual esteem of their fellow-creatures, is strong and ineradicable. What an agonising dilemma Baudelaire reveals when he confesses that "even as a child I found in my heart twin contradictory sentiments: the horror of life and an ecstasy of living. . . . C'est bien le fait", he adds, "d'un paresseux nerveux". But whether that last comment be fair or no, his dilemma, we must admit, is also a characteristic of the entire range of modern poetry. His verse is a spark flashing between positive and negative poles; his sense of aloofness is only less urgent than his sense of being ineluctably attached to a world whose values he rejects and by whom he too is rejected. And just as Tolstoy, deeply sunk in the bitterness of a perverse dogma, could glance up at the apparition of a pair of belted and helmeted Russian guardsmen and discover in their stupidity, unawakened subservience and the gross healthiness of their features something touching and significant, an indescribable charm which nearly moved him to tears, so Baudelaire, and more generously, was always prepared to establish an emotional contact with a world of appearances he despised. Like other masters of the literary expression of the nineteenth century, Baudelaire was disturbed and profoundly alienated by the disastrous encroachment of feminism. Feminine chicanery, we know, he had good reason to distrust; and feminine directness and much-vaunted practical *flair* struck painfully on a temperament whose apparent evasiveness was rooted in an intense delicacy of feeling:

> Woman (he declared in *Mon Cœur Mis à Nu*) is the antithesis of the Dandy.   Hence she should inspire horror.
> She is hungry, and she must eat; thirsty, and she must drink.
> . . . Woman is *natural*, that is to say, abominable.

Feminine intellectualism—as well it might be—was even more abhorrent. Of George Sand,—parenthetically "cette latrine!"—he notes that "she is unintelligent, crass, talkative. In the region of moral ideas, she has the same depth of judgment and the same refinement of emotion as concierges and kept-women." Yet, in spite of this extreme repugnance, it was among women that, while age and illness were gradually sapping the superficial aspect of his dandyism, Baudelaire chiefly looked for consolation and support, and towards several women,—towards his mother, towards the memory of Mariette, Madame Sabatier and the mysterious Marie X. . . ,—that he projected those last desperate sallies of feeling, as superbly pure and disinterested as they were evidently foredoomed to failure.

But Mariette was dead; and Madame Baudelaire met his appeals with an unfailing tenderness, still with an equally unfailing lack of comprehension. The episode of Marie X. . . . is obscure and the anecdote of Madame Sabatier must be reserved for a later paragraph. Meantime, let me review Baudelaire's situation as it might have appeared, say five years previous to his death,—on the twenty-third of January, 1862,—a date I have chosen because it was on that day Baudelaire committed to his journal a peculiar and terrible entry: "Aujourd'hui j'ai subi un singulier avertissement, j'ai senti passer sur moi le vent de l'aile de l'imbécillité." Follows, under a new heading, *Hygiène, Morale*, the resolution to escape to his mother's "doll's house" at Honfleur: "A Honfleur! le plus tôt possible, avant de tomber plus bas." It was a resolution, we know, which Baudelaire did not keep. Honfleur and the house above the cliffs, with its promise of tranquillity, of health and spiritual well-being, beckoned him, but Paris, though he hated it and hated his life there, had witnessed the inception of his miseries, had been the theatre of his success; the associations it contained had wound him in far tougher bonds than, strain against them as he liked, he could ever break through. So in Paris he stayed. A month earlier, he had made a final, despairing effort to reinstate himself in public opinion and reap some small material benefit from twenty years of toil, which if it had been intermittent had, at least, been continuously and obstinately resumed. His intention, no doubt, was largely to please his mother; she must have something she could tell her neighbours, some object for the innocent self-congratulation without which no mother's happiness is entire. General Aupick was dead; Baudelaire dallied with the thought that he and his mother might recapture that period of mutual devotion which her second marriage had interrupted. But first, he must achieve this supreme vindication of his labours, and he began canvassing for the Academic Chair recently vacated by the death of Eugène Scribe. It was an absurd, a hopeless task, and when he had finally abandoned it, looking back across the years of disillusion and disappointment, Baudelaire may have thought that the series of his humiliations was now complete. We need hardly remember his reverses in detail; there had been, for instance, the Family Council which took the control of his income out of his own hands. It was a necessary step, but how acutely painful, how galling! Then, in 1857, *Les Fleurs du Mal* had been condemned as obscene. There was an accumulating load of debt and the recollection of innumerable, sometimes shifty, sometimes frankly dishonest sleights to which he had resorted in the hope of alleviating it; Ancelle, the notary who paid his monthly allowance, had raised so many obstacles, and Baudelaire had whipped himself into such futile rages and almost spat into the old man's face, departing furiously, only to be obliged to return, humbled and suppliant, next week . . .

He had experienced, too, another and more intimate kind of failure. Between 1852 and 1857, between the thirty-first and thirty-sixth years of his age, Baudelaire despatched anonymously a large number of letters and poems to a house in the *rue Frochot* where he had occasionally dined. Its occupant was a Madame Sabatier, known as *La Présidente* and the centre of a noisy, amorous group of friends which included Flaubert and Gautier.[1] Madame Sabatier was a rather coarse, entirely good-hearted woman, who lived amid her companions upon terms of the utmost sexual bonhômie. She was good-natured and accessible, yet Baudelaire preferred to approach her with the infinite precautions, the

---

[1] For a different and more agreeable view of *La Présidente*, see the second volume of Judith Gautier's Memoirs: her kindliness, her gaiety, her courage under misfortune,—"elle faisait sa cuisine elle-même, en chantant, des turquoises à ses jolies mains, le petit doigt relevé . . ."

wealth of delicacy he might have been justified in employing if *La Présidente* had been a Virgin or a Muse. Eventually, after five years' procrastination, he declared himself and, since at that time the condemnation of *Les Fleurs du Mal* had made him temporarily famous, was accepted without more ado. The contact was unfortunate; his idol had "become a woman", Baudelaire cried, precipitately retiring behind a shower of elusively worded missives in which he protests his devotion and hints at the inadvisability of their encounter ever being renewed. It was precisely satisfaction, and satisfaction so gross and so whole-hearted, that he had wished to avoid. Similarly, we notice a triumphant inflection in the long passionate letter he addressed to Madame Marie X. . . . after she had refused his suit. He is glad, yes, glad of her refusal. This is an enjoyment he recognises, an atmosphere he can breathe. His genius is at home in the atmosphere of excessive, unqualified sexuality exhaled by Jeanne's presence; he understands and enjoys the animal commerce and appreciates the ferocious spontaneity of the partner with whom it is shared. He has come to appreciate, more and more keenly, a devotion that does not subsist upon the shifting balance of appetites. It is the contemplative devotion—"Par vous, Marie," he writes, "je serai fort et grand . . ." It is the devotion which, M. Charles du Bos remarks, has only need of a contemplative assuagement,—"qui ne possède vraiment que parce qu'il ne possède pas".

Together with the need for abstinence, rises the need for prayer. Baudelaire's strong Christian tendency has, I think, of late been somewhat overemphasised. "Quand même dieu n'existerait pas" (he wrote at the beginning of *Fusées*), "la religion serait encore sainte et divine." Further than that, it seems, he could never find it in his reason to go. "Je suis mystique au fond et je ne crois à rien," M. du Bos recalls Flaubert's confession. In Baudelaire's scheme, the regular exercise of daily prayer should have introduced the regular discipline of systematised work and amusement, which, all his life through, he had tried and failed to achieve. Its purpose was *disciplinary*; God was a receptacle of prayers, and prayer a *magic* operation. Still, pray he did, using the simplest form of words: "Ne me châtiez pas dans ma mère et ne châtiez pas ma mère à cause de moi.—Je vous recommande les âmes de mon père et de Mariette.—Donnez-moi la force de faire immédiatement mon devoir tous les jours et de devenir ainsi un héros et un saint." The simplicity of that address recalls the consummate simplicity with which he strips himself bare in the letters written to his mother. "With you", he interjects, "I can have no false shame" . . . So it is the naked man he reveals. All pretences are abandoned. Then, by prayer, he hopes, this state of grace may be perpetuated. Again, he flings away all artifice, whether it is the artifice of a writer, of the man accustomed to decorate and exploit his emotions, or the artifice of pride. He determines that he will solve his problems by reducing them to their very simplest causes; and, as a last sacrifice casting aside any trace of spiritual vanity, he confines his intercessions to the humble requirements of a modest and laborious career.

And the background of Baudelaire's development? It is a background of urban civilisation. Writers habituated to the agglomeration of hovels, merchants' houses and palaces recently named a city, sprawled along the banks of some quiet-flowing river, traversing here and there its crumbling circuit of walls and spreading out in pleasantly gardened suburbs which ended abruptly before the limitless prospect of empty, uncontaminated coppices and fields, could have but little conception of the city as it has grown up within the last hundred years, and might probably fail to understand how intense a focus of emotional disturbance the modern city has become. Examine the London and suburban landscapes of Rowlandson or Hogarth and reflect,—in spite of the business and glamour of the market scenes, the uproarious concourse of vehicles delivering their passengers, amid flocks being driven in to slaughter, coaches with locked wheels, while women toss the contents of their chamber-pots over the heads of drunken gentlemen struggling home after a carouse, —upon the tranquil, rustic air of the London they delineate. It is a country town, no worse, crowded during market day. Then, perhaps,—mounting one of the northern eminences, past Lambeth's venerable shades and so up into suburbs which almost within living memory were a region of wild, hilly wood-land,—look backwards and to right and left through the smoky branches of a few still-standing elms and survey whole districts quite unknown to the traveller even by reputation—an interminable perspective of dusky houses piled ridge behind ridge, the shining asphalt of public playgrounds, the huge metal disc of an isolated reservoir, dark clusters of factory chim-neys and the ineffective insurgence of blackened neo-Gothic spires. Here the very wind smells alien, but the murmur of distant traffic, the harsh, grinding noise of brakes, reminds us that the strange terri-tories lying at our feet are only an extension, the parasitic outer growth of districts with which we are more familiar. These streets run with the same life; the same central pulse animates them. For, sluggish and apparently inert, the entire polypus-mass is awake with a horrid indestructible tenacity. Streets and houses die; their window-panes are broken, and soiled newspapers and discarded wrappings silt up against the doorsteps or drift languidly down into the areas. Presently they will be renewed; and meanwhile, like those unsightly defences with which a human body protects its reparatory operations, a scab of placards, hoardings and moist and wrinkled play-bills covers up the temporary breach. Then, as the modern poet, Baudelaire let us say, or another and lesser poet from the host of his literary descendants, Jules Laforgue or Mallarmé, wanders past, —born *flâneurs* that they all of them were,—peering up and noticing the damp, corrugated surface of the advertisements, though he may experience and record his personal "immense nausée des affiches", he also experiences a sense of immense exaltation; he feels that inward quiver of disgust and excitement with which every healthy organism responds to the idea of change.

Baudelaire saw Paris change all around him, but not gradually and stealthily as other cities have changed. The new builders cut their way into antiquity, like a mower cutting a swathe through a field of tall grass. New avenues and new boulevards were opened; old quarters disappeared in dust and rubble:

> Le vieux Paris n'est plus (la forme d'une ville
> Change plus vite, hélas! que le cœur d'un mortel) . . .

A new commerce, spectacularly described many years later in Zola's *Au Bonheur des Dames*, displaced the old and imposed new fashions, more in keeping with the prodigal spirit of the age. A crinoline demands twice as much silk as was required to make up the decent amplitude of flounced and pleated skirt worn in the 'thirties. But then, for a poet, and especially for Baudelaire, who had announced that he found all fashions "delightful—*relatively* delightful, that is to say", an atmosphere of profusion, of luxury and competitive elegance, can never cease to be inspiriting. *Odi et amo*—I hate and, if I had my wish, would exclude women from churches and from the gatherings of intelligent men; nevertheless, in my capacity of poet, I am bound to confess that I "take as keen a pleasure in the *mundus muliebris*", I mean the complete apparatus of decorative deceits and artificial, money-bought attractions, "as women do themselves".—It is, in fact, the *topical quality* which has enslaved his imagination; "the beautiful", he had written, prefacing his study of Constantin Guys, "is composed of an *eternal* element whose quantity it is extremely difficult to assess and of a *relative*, *circumstantial* element, *qui sera, si l'on veut, tour à tour ou tout ensemble, l'époque, la mode, la morale, la passion*". And so the spectacle holds while it also repels him; and if the Second Empire and its vulgar faiths—"Les brigands seuls sont convaincus,—de quoi?—Qu'il leur faut réussir . . ."—and proportionately vulgar scepticism—"Je m'ennuie en France, surtout parce que tout le monde y ressemble à Voltaire" (or, as he might have written half a century later: à M. Anatole France)—was hardly calculated to please a writer who, after losing all taste for proletarian upheavals during his half-hearted participation in the street-fighting of 1848, had become the visionary advocate of aristocratic government, still, at least, it did bring in its train a certain abundance, a certain heavy and full-blown profusion in the styles of architecture, manners and dress:

> Quand tu vas balayant l'air de ta jupe large,
>> Tu fais l'effet d'un beau vaisseau qui prend le large,
>>> Chargé de toile, et va roulant
>> Suivant un rhythme doux, et paresseux, et lent . . .

—the new, denationalised, flaring gas-lit Paris provided him with a sense of sleepless, feverish activity, which he likened to a movement through the streets of soldiers hurrying out to strike some treacherous, concerted blow:

>> A travers les lueurs que tourmente le vent
>> La Prostitution s'allume dans les rues;
>> Comme une fourmilière elle ouvre ses issues.
>> Partout elle se fraye, un occulte chemin,
>> Ainsi que l'ennemi qui tente un coup de main . . .

For no poet has given us a more literal transcript of his surroundings than Baudelaire, nor contrived to elevate his "realism" on to so high a plane of fantasy. I have already noticed an incidental resemblance to

THE CRINOLINE: Drawing by Constantin Guys

the *English Opium-Eater*;—both De Quincey and Baudelaire were addicts of laudanum and haschish; according to the varying degrees of their genius, each was oppressed by the nightmare of metropolitan civilisation. And then each writer, too, has put it on record how the workings of the drug sharpened and subtilised his apprehension of the outside world. In a celebrated passage of *Les Paradis artificiels* Baudelaire recounts what is apparently the common experience of drug-takers,—pleasures and pains enormously intensified, the evidence of the separate senses confused, sounds visible, colours audible, accompanied by so violent a dislocation of the temporal sense that the dragging moments of a wintry afternoon seem to promise, as they limp past, not so much an eventual release from tedium as an eternity of imprisonment:

> Rien n'égale en longueur les boiteuses journées,
> Quand sous les lourds flocons des neigeuses années
> L'Ennui, fruit de la morne incuriosité,
> Prend les proportions de l'immortalité.

Then, sleep seems, not a refuge, but a gulf, a bottomless, cavernous aperture which it is his nightly misfortune to traverse; and furthermore, he wrote, "upon the moral plane as upon the physical, I have always had the sensation of a yawning gulf, not only the gulf of sleep, but the gulf of action, the gulf of rêverie, the gulf of recollection, of desire, of regret, of

remorse, of the beautiful, of numbers, and so forth
. . ." From this point a short excursion of memory
will serve to bring back the lines in which he writes
of himself as seated—

> . . . au fond d'un théâtre banal
> Qu'enflammait l'orchestre sonore.

Colder than an ice-cave he has described his situation in *Les Paradis*, and the drug-taker transfixed
there as cold as if his body were fashioned from a
solid block of ice. Yet, out of the sonorous concave
of the orchestra springs a rush of sound, translated
under his eyes into spires and rolling gushes of
flame; the music is a *conflagration*; even the hallucina-
tory effects of the drug make their contribution to
the surpassing richness and intricacy of his verse.

*   *   *

I have attempted the portrait of a man, for whom
the completeness of his life could only be expressed
in the apparent incompleteness of its results. For
such a traveller, there is no *end*, no justificatory *conclusion*, to his labours. Conclusions are reached by
compromise; the problem he had essayed was of its
very nature insoluble. Though the path he had been
following—with so much difficulty, with so many
hesitations—had seemed to lead him to one of those
doubtful places where there are footsteps and con-

flicting wheel-marks but no clear assurance of the road, it was the same path which a little later his successors and disciples resumed; the direction in which Charles Baudelaire first guided our interest is a direction from which a modern poet, however unwilling or incompetent, finds it impossible to turn aside.

Here was the Dandy personified. And what is it, this being of whose name I have made such loose and unscrupulous employment? The adversary of life, then, the impassioned critic of himself and of his fellows, who is also their impassioned and poetic advocate,—the artist suspended in doubtful eminence by the thrust of two contradictory powers; he is divided between the claims of contemplation and action; he is obsessed by the meanness of his own abilities and by the surpassing greatness of his designs; he is greedy of life and happiness, yet amorous of suffering and dissolution. He is a type anticipated in the plays of Elizabethan dramatists,[1] in the verses of seventeenth-century poets, and partially explored in the novels of Stendhal and Lermontov,—a veritable *Hero of Our Time*, as Lermontov chose to call his book. For he is our chief Accuser of the modern world, yet he is also its most patriotic citizen;—we are hedged in by a ring of painful anomalies; he runs

[1] See Wyndham Lewis, *The Lion and the Fox*, page 184 and elsewhere.

forward and, like a sheaf of spears, gathers them into his own bosom.

In generalisation though, we need not lose sight of the Dandy's historic antecedents, nor blind ourselves to the fact that this phenomenon we brand as the "modern poet" is a phenomenon as frequently recurring as the set of conditions which engender it. While the life-forces of a nation or a continent run into its capital cities, while commerce prospers at the expense of agriculture, finance at the expense of aristocracy, then in the microcosm of the poet's constitution a corresponding process of centralisation appears to take place. His apprehensions, perhaps, are no less keen, still the range of his sympathies is far less wide; or say that, if he notices more than his predecessors, what he notices is far more remote from himself. His content and manner are more abstruse than theirs, yet he also allows his verse an occasional homeliness, an immediacy of expression that an elder poet would have lacked the daring necessary to venture. Thus Catullus had introduced a certain colloquialism into the grammatical framework and the vocabulary of his poems, and first learned to charge with ironic significance some startling or bathetic piece of imagery:

> Caeli, Lesbia nostra, Lesbia illa,
> illa Lesbia, quam Catullus unam
> plus quam se atque suos amavit omnes,

CHARLES BAUDELAIRE

nunc in quadriviis et angiportis
glubit magnanimi Remi nepotes.

And so Baudelaire, too (we have Jules Laforgue's
authority for stating), was he who "first after the
hardihood of the Romantic school, discovered those
crude comparisons—qui soudain dans l'harmonie
d'une période mettent en passant le pied dans le plat:
comparaisons palpables, trop premier plan, en un mot
américaines semble-t-il" . . . Thus in Baudelaire's
verse the fabulous Island of Love is merely—

> . . . un pays fameux dans les chansons,
> Eldorado banal de tous les vieux garçons.
> Regardez, après tout, c'est une pauvre terre.

Or, having launched another poem with the brief
Racinian invocation:

> Andromaque, je pense à vous!

as if intending to revisit the immobile dignity of
ancient sorrows, thereafter he lets the wind of the
present fill his sails and, along an easy and majestic
course, waft him home between the familiar, fetid
quays:

> Je pense à la négresse, amaigrie et phtisique,
> Piétinant dans la boue, et cherchant, l'œil hagard,
> Les cocotiers absents de la superbe Afrique
> Derrière la muraille immense du brouillard.
>
> .   .   .   .   .   .
>
> Ainsi dans la forêt où mon esprit s'exile
> Un vieux Souvenir sonne à plein souffle du cor!

57

Je pense aux matelots oubliés dans une île,
Aux captifs, aux vaincus! . . . à bien d'autres encore!

Equally characteristic of his method are the large
and ostensibly careless gesture with which he concludes his theme, as though the images he propounds
were spread for a moment under our eyes and immediately rolled up again and thrust away, accompanied by the exclamation, impatient or weary, that
there are still others, many, many of them—

. . . bien d'autres encore!

which he has not the heart to unfold,—and his habit
of permitting us to distinguish such heroic and
radiant symbols as his imagination may suggest only
in the perspective of regret or through the transparency of present sorrow. It is through the curtains
of Parisian fog that the apparition of her own superb
continent confronts the negress; he writes of An-
dromache, not fresh and firm-breasted, holding
Astyanax in her arms, as she parted from Hector in
the shadow of the Skaian gate, but of her gigantic
reflection thrown across the dull glass of a wintry
northern river. And, all the time, persuasive and
indefatigable, he draws the reader closer to the
surface of his poem, now detailed and pedantic,
now seeming to extend his scope till it includes
the widest possible range of human suffering:

. . . quiconque a perdu ce qui ne se retrouve . . .

58

bidding him recognise there himself, intimately pleading with him that he will recognise and acknowledge the bond of common experience which unites them—

> Tu le connais, lecteur . . .

overcoming this resistance, or, no doubt, giving him a final contemptuous permission to ignore the kinship if he dares, flinging him back into the futurity from which he has momentarily plucked him forth:

> Tu le connais, lecteur, ce monstre délicat,
> — Hypocrite lecteur,—mon semblable,—mon frère!

Then, whether he is resentful or he is willing, a reader must necessarily admit the *completeness* of this universe in which he has been engulfed by the poet. Other poetic systems, he may argue, are in comparison either the product of borrowed and gradually perfected aesthetic artifice, or else seem to have been built upon some scaffolding of faith or alien "philosophy" which has since rotted and fallen away, leaving the poetical structure intact. This universe is centralised, though its firmament is low and weighs heavily over the head:

> Le ciel bas et lourd pèse comme un couvercle . . .

like an unfathomable autumn landscape, he admires its profundity (has not Baudelaire described the "sensation du gouffre" which, he said, inhabited him?)

and admires still more the independence and boldness of the informing spirit, ambushed in its midst,
which, by the simple power of the word, has elicited
from Chaos an entire cosmic illusion of sombre and
almost colourless magnificence.[1] For many poets, as
Jehovah did upon the sacred mountain, have con-
jured up a semblance, as it were, a broken fragment of
"paved work of sapphire-stone" under their feet, but
how few of them stand firmly and can claim a perfect
consistency and regularity of design in the world of
images they have created! To that basic consistency
I must refer again later. Meanwhile, observe the
suppleness of his reach, the rapidity with which he
can move to and fro betwixt extreme quarters of the
horizon.

Our poet, we remember, loved the dryness, spare-
ness, and classical monotony which is peculiar to
true elegance, and found his ideal elegance best
summed up in the tight-rigged image of a modern
sailing-ship. Appealing in itself, the attraction of the
ship is also implicit in the enormous diversity of
images its contemplation suggests; the more precise
the form, the greater its wealth of associations. It is

---

[1] Dis-moi, mon âme, pauvre âme refroidie, que penserais-tu
d'habiter Lisbonne? . . . Cette ville est au bord de l'eau; on dit qu'elle
est bâtie en marbre, et que le peuple y a une telle haine du végétal, qu'il
arrache tous les arbres. Voilà un paysage selon ton goût; un paysage
fait avec la lumière et le minéral, et le liquide pour les réfléchir! *Any-
where out of the world.—Petits Poëmes en prose.*

anchored; it lies becalmed; or its sails flap and crack and belly, and it runs forward into the unknown, dwindling till it seems no larger than a nautilus-shell, dragging behind it as it flies a fine-drawn vanishing thread of nostalgic sentiment:

> Dis-moi, ton cœur parfois s'envole-t-il, Agathe,
> Loin du noir océan de l'immonde cité,
> Vers un autre océan où la splendeur éclate,
> Bleu, clair, profond, ainsi que la virginité?

Bearing that image in mind, bearing in mind, too, the nature of the temperament which had conceived it, we shall be prepared to realise and, realising, to account for the extraordinary flexibility of Baudelaire's poetic style. We shall understand its defects,—its harshness, its occasional rather acrid pedantry, its rhetorical excess of emphasis; we shall be able to reconcile his *classicism*,—his revival, that is to say, of the splendours of precise and didactic statement, —with his achievement of a lyrical and *romantic* utterance carried to its furthest and most nebulous point of attenuation. Baudelaire's classicism—and the attempted classicism of modern poets in general —is the alliance of an extreme lyrical suggestiveness and an extreme, even dogmatic, clarity:

> Pour l'enfant, amoureux de cartes et d'estampes,
> L'univers est égal à son vaste appétit.
> Ah! que le monde est grand à la clarté des lampes!
> Aux yeux du souvenir que le monde est petit!

Pitched in whatever key, his poems never quite forget the resonant undertone, the rhythmic, sententious gravity of Latin verse.

It remains now to scrutinise the example of Baudelaire's career as it affected his immediate successors, and to explain how it is that, far from diminishing, his influence upon the modern poet daily grows stronger and more important. There has sprung up of late a dissatisfaction with Romanticism, aimed not so much against the obvious inequalities of its products, its frequent lapses, the curious aural insensitiveness its exponents so often display, as against the essential instability of the whole fabric. Its basis is unsound. These men, we feel, were distinguished by a kind of brilliant puerility; they were "winning"; they were personally delightful; they whored after Causes; they dreamed of the instantaneous perfectibility of the human race; and it is as hard to feel sympathy for their inevitable and bitter disappointment as it is hard to console the lover who, when he has spent long months seeking a convenient object for his passion, pretends that Love caught him unawares and, unasked, dealt him a treacherous and irremediable blow. Of right, wrongness, truth, error, we need make no question, but shall call our standards *honesty* and *dishonesty* instead. To the creative artist any and every idea may be relatively valuable; his *treatment* of the idea concerns

62

us, since a sterile course of intellectual philanderings cannot do other than recoil unfavourably upon the prospects of his work. Then, in spite of the manifold contradictions they enclose,—his pedantry, the misplaced emphasis with which he sometimes wrote,—the volumes of Baudelaire's critical essays and the notebook volume of critical and autobiographical jottings represent a singularly consistent attitude and an equipoise of praise and blame which, even though one day we come precisely to reverse the balance, will still seem, I believe, to have been very honestly and scrupulously weighed. I have cited his eulogy of Constantin Guys; I must include his championship of Manet and frenetic admiration of Delacroix. He was also a fervent Wagnerian,—and, if that last connection is measurably less sympathetic to us than the others, we should remember, as M. Jean Cocteau has pointed out, that, at the time and granted the character of the opposing armies, his partisanship was proper and unavoidable.[1]

He had been, in fact, one of those rare critical intelligences, possessed of a natural aptitude for what is best and most hopeful among their contemporaries' work,—such men as, amid the hurly-burly of contemporary enthusiasm and disdain, have an in-

---

[1] Lorsque Baudelaire a défendu Wagner, il faisait de l'opposition aristocratique. Il n'y avait pas d'autre attitude possible.—*Le Coq et l'Arlequin.*

stinctive leaning towards the few, usually depressed and neglected, figures who will afterwards seem to have been the giants of the age in which they lived. He had enjoyed a *sense of his own age*, had recognised its pattern while the pattern was yet incomplete, and —because it is only our misapprehension of the present which prevents our looking into the immediate future, our ignorance of to-day and of its real as apart from its spurious tendencies and requirements—had anticipated many problems, both on the aesthetic and on the moral plane, in which the fate of modern poetry is still concerned. For Baudelaire's achievement is a kind of dividing range or watershed, down whose flanks the lesser, less strictly original, less adventurous talents of the generation which followed him were able to take their individual ways, each of them choosing a different aspect of the central pile, each closely indebted to the recollection of his genius. Thus, Villiers de l'Isle-Adam was to accentuate and even parody the attitude of aristocratic opposition with which Baudelaire had fronted the world; Tristan Corbière to exemplify and exaggerate the intransigeance of his dandyhood, of the Romantic outcast who is so radically disabused that he has, incidentally, lost faith in Romanticism. His irony was Jules Laforgue's province; and here, if the disparity of magnitude is most obviously marked, there was also, perhaps, the strongest correspondence of intellectual and spiritual traits. Laforgue's was a small talent, you may object, and sedulously limited. It is in the scrupulous limitation of its own talents that the true measure of modern heroism sometimes consists.

GÉRARD DE NERVAL

WAKING from one of those spells of madness into which he dropped off as quickly and almost as noiselessly as though he were falling asleep,—that is to say if you imagine sleep on every occasion gathering a little added power, prolonging itself a little further, and a drowsy film gradually encroaching on his wakeful life,—Gérard de Nerval was amused but apparently unastonished to find his obsequies already performed. Like an inscribed sheet of heavy white marble, Dumas *père* had laid an appreciative testimony on his grave. "*C'est un esprit charmant*" . . . he read the characters. Grammatical accuracy might impose the present tense, but there was no mistaking the valedictory turn of the composition. It was the year 1854. And he wrote dedicating a new book, *Les Filles de Feu*, a volume which included *Sylvie*, to his recovered friend. "I am dedicating this book to you, my dear master," he wrote, "just as I dedicated *Lorely* to Jules Janin. I had the same reason for gratitude. Some years ago, I was supposed to be dead, and he wrote my biography. Some days ago, I was supposed to be mad, and you dedicated some of your most charming lines by way of epitaph on my intelligence. See what glory has reached me before my hour." Then, as if he wanted none of the comedy of the situation to escape him, he proceeded with the recapitulation of Alexandre Dumas's opaque, well-intentioned phrases: "un esprit charmant et distingué ... chez lequel, de temps en temps, un certain phénomène se produit. ... Lorsqu'un travail quelconque l'a fort préoccupé, l'imagination, cette folle du logis, en chasse momentanément la raison ... et alors ... le jette dans les théories impossibles, dans les livres infaisables." With much else, celebrating Gérard's extraordinary narrative gift, which the divagations of his mind and body only served to nourish, that is the pith of Dumas's contorted sentence, the tribute of an inferior mind, yet a mind presumably eminent enough to realise the superiority of its subject, Gérard's superiority over and above the facile evaluation which would have excused his dismissal,—the "original", the eccentric talker whose achievement lay interred among the dust of a thousand forgotten conversations.

But, removing his scrutiny from Dumas's epitaph, "Je vais essayer de vous expliquer, mon cher Dumas, le phénomène dont vous avez parlé plus haut", Gérard continued. The explanation leads so direct to the centre of his achievement, and so inevitably to the centre of his personal life, that a short détour is necessary. A vigorous desire towards the impersonal will find it hard to separate the work of Gérard

Labrunie, "le bon Gérard",—Gérard de Nerval he preferred to call himself,—from the circumstances and ultimate catastrophe of his life. Still, there will be no need, I think, to allow his remark, that he arranged his life as if it were a novel, any predominantly serious value. After all, those arrangements are not uncommon. An arranged life generally resembles some grotesque libretto, where the music is lacking or rises quite inaudibly except for the ear of its composer. And the intention, the arranging passions run precisely counter to the artist's true direction. They prompt a stirring up of the lees, exaltation of the resultant hazy cloud, while the artist waits its subsidence till he can run off a translucent, clarified liquor.

As a writer, if Gérard failed, it was not because he had wilfully infringed any of the conditions which ought to surround an artist's work. So momentous was his work, that, insensibly, it submerged and half obliterated the ordinary considerations of his life. Physiological weakness I must leave out of account. Since I cannot determine its source or probable effects, I must assume that it merely heightened his intellectual tendency. The distinction between "real" and "imaginary" shapes was obscured. Mainly in accordance with the latter he was inclined to regulate his movements. And he failed as an artist, just so far as it is impossible wholly to strip his work from the objects about which it took shape. Say that, like

68

the Pompeian ash, it carries, embedded in its mass,
the hollow casts or impressions of several part real,
part imaginary personalities.

Part real—for his innate waywardness did not
admit of a figure enjoying different degrees of significance in two different spheres. Figures, which
engaged his attention, were straightway borne over
by him and pinnacled in the sphere of art. Elsewhere,
they no longer existed. You would be hard put to it
to recall another writer who even attempted such a
complete transubstantiation, unless it was, perhaps,
Blake. And, on both occasions, the poet, pure artist
as intentions went, thus burdened his art with immense irregularities and imperfections. Excepting a
single further trait, which will find its context later,
there the resemblance ends. Gérard's life was made
much easier, and the practice of his art a great deal
more difficult, by the chance possession of a sort of
loquacious ease or mechanical exuberance. He had
the courage and the insensitiveness to collaborate
with Alexandre Dumas at operettas and verse-plays.
Nor was Dumas his sole collaborator. He employed
his aptitude in the confection of newspaper articles
and feuilletons, when a couple of small patrimonies,
brought into his hands from his mother, who died on
the Russian campaign, and from the learned uncle
in whose household he grew up, had dwindled
away to nothing.

Gérard had dissipated his fortune, Théophile Gautier declared, in an orgy of canes and in a debauch of opera-glasses. He must have new canes, so that he could beat a louder and more various thunder of applause on the floor of the *parterre*, where for some long time he appeared, the opening sentences of *Sylvie* inform us, "en grande tenue de soupirant". Curiously innocent of the narrowest kind of personal feeling, this obsession claims a record, because it occupied a place that might have been filled, say, by the habits of a metaphysical apprenticeship or by a prepossession with scientific research. I mean it altered and pointed his characteristic imagery. Besides, at that period, covered by the pontificate of Scribe, the period of the *Tour de Nesle*,—Hugo, Vigny, Musset and their essentially undramatic products looming like turbulent cloud-shapes, which never brought rain,—though the fountain-head of drama was nearly parched, opposed springs, no doubt deriving from the same subterranean river of delight, poured forth a muddier illusion.

> . . . Lesser nymphs on sides of hills
> From plaything urns pour down their rills.

And the vulgarities of the contemporary vaudeville and music-hall, a slight stream of art coiling and lacing among its accumulated ordures, "les détritus des serres, les décatis bouquets de galas éphémères", which the nineteenth-century Hamlet surveyed out of the window of his speculative sentinel-tower, began to flow like a Jordan, curative for its very filth:

> J'ai vu parfois, au fond d'un théâtre banal
> Qu'enflammait l'orchestre sonore,
> Une fée allumer dans un ciel infernal
> Une miraculeuse aurore;
> J'ai vu parfois, au fond d'un théâtre banal
>
> Un être qui n'était que lumière, or et gaze
> Terrasser l'énorme Satan . . .

Here, Gérard, a smaller poet, resorted, too. The nightly spectacle, futile and charming, made a peculiar modification of his sensibility. And he must have new opera-glasses, because each new pair might draw the spectacle closer. But he required a lens, clearer,—yet subtly warping,—than the optician was competent to supply. As it has frequently happened, the absence of a mechanical satisfaction flung him back on his own ingenuity.

Eventually I return to Gérard's promised explanation. "I am going to try to explain to you, my dear Dumas, the phenomenon of which you have spoken above." He commenced a leisurely unrolling: "Certain story-tellers, you know, are bound to identify themselves, while they go along, with the creatures of their proper imagination. You remember our old friend, Nodier, describing how he had had the ill-luck to be guillotined during the Terror.

... Well—you must believe me—the excitement of composition may produce a kindred effect. . . . That is exactly what has happened to me through undertaking the history of a personage who played his part, I think, about the epoch of Louis Quinze, under the pseudonym of Brisacier. Where can I have read the disastrous biography of this adventurer?" The undiscoverable biography became an obsession, and, presently, a recollected apothegm was sharpening his torments:

Inventer, au fond, c'est se ressouvenir. . . . Since I was unable to come upon any proof of my hero's material existence, behold me no less firmly convinced of the transmigration of spirits than, say, Pythagoras or Pierre Leroux. . . . From the moment when I seemed to have recaptured the series of my previous existences, it needed but a short stretch of imagination to persuade myself that I had been prince, king, hierophant and even god; the chain was broken and minutes had now become hours. Could I condense my recollections into a masterpiece, it is a new Dream of Scipio I should write, another Tasso's Vision or Divine Comedy of Dante. Putting aside once and for all, though, any pretension to the glory of inspired, illuminist or prophetic spirit, I can only offer you what you so justly call *des théories impossibles, un livre infaisable,* of which here is the opening chapter, the continuation, it might appear, of Scarron's *Roman Comique.* . . . Judge of it for me.

But the chapter which follows is probably indebted, not so much to Scarron's tedious novel, as to the abundant declamatory passages of Heine's

Reisebilder. Gérard had made a prose translation of
some of Heine's poems, and it was on Heine's door
he had knocked a year earlier, heralding the Last
Judgement. The unfinished *Roman Tragique* repres-
ents "l'illustre Brisacier", charlatan prince who has
joined a troupe of comedians, penniless at a country
inn, abandoned by the actress he loved. "Ainsi, moi,
le brillant comédien naguère, *le prince ignoré, l'amant
mystérieux, le déshérité, le banni de liesse, le beau ténébreux* . . . je n'ai pas été mieux traité que ce pauvre
Ragotin, un poéterau de province, un robin!" . . .
Constellation of epithets, restrung and brilliantly
fixed in the verse of *El Desdichado*! And quickly we
recognise that Gérard has annexed Brisacier's rôle.
The supposed narrative employs a letter-form, and
I hazard a suggestion, so strangely does Brisacier's
letter resemble several fragmentary letters, printed
at the end of *Le Rêve et la Vie*, that an appeal to a
living person may have provided its grounding.

Aurélia Brisacier's actress was called, a name of
special connotation for Gérard. When he had served
his novice term of canes and opera-glasses, Gérard,
like Brisacier, had accompanied a troupe of actors,
making the round of provincial theatres. He had
assisted them in their performances. "Vous souve-
nez-vous de la façon dont je jouais Achille, quand,
par hasard, passant dans une ville de troisième ou de
quatrième ordre, il nous prenait la fantaisie d'étendre

le culte négligé des anciens tragiques français?
J'étais noble et puissant, n'est-ce pas, sous le casque
doré aux crins de pourpre, sous la cuirasse étin-
celante?" . . . That was the story current among
Gérard's large acquaintance, to whom his adventures
were the source of pity, consternation, and yet,
naturally, of perennial entertainment. Again, we
have the evidence of *Sylvie*, and the anecdote has
been repeated by M. Gauthier Ferrières, in a biographical study, published twenty years ago.

An excessively complete identification of himself
with his protagonist drove upwards, towards the
light, minute swarming recollections, where they
burst with a sort of partisan vehemence and acri-
mony. "Un sifflet, un sifflet indigne, *sous ses yeux*,
près d'elle, à cause d'elle! Un sifflet qu'elle s'attribue
—par ma faute (comprenez bien!), et vous deman-
derez ce qu'on fait quand on tient la foudre! . . . Oh!
tenez, mes amis! J'ai eu un moment l'idée d'être vrai,
d'être grand, de me faire immortel enfin, sur votre
théâtre de planches et de toiles, et dans votre comédie
d'oripeaux!" He had only to detach a *quinquet*, apply
it to the canvas of the wings, and consume theatre and
audience alike! But detailed recapitulation answers
no purpose. The feverish narrative hurries on, to an
inconclusive conclusion, and, after a nominal full-
stop, Gérard, though in a rather less measured and
colloquial tone, takes up again his explanatory labour:

Once persuaded that it was my own history I was writing,
I set myself to work transcribing therein all my dreams, all
my emotions. I grew tender, musing upon this passion of
mine for a falling star that passed and left me disconsolate,
alone in the black night of my destiny. I wept; I shuddered
before the empty apparitions of my sleep. Then, across my
torments, shone a divinely merciful ray. Encompassed by
monstrous shapes, against whom I kept up a shadowy war-
fare, I seized Ariadne's thread and thereafter all my visions
took on a celestial mildness. Some day I shall endite the
narrative of this descent into the nether regions, and you will
perceive that, though mad, my madness has not always lacked
a kind of method.

Clues and mysterious references back and forth!
But my projected survey, too long anchored above
a single date, the year 1854, preceding the year of
Gérard's death, though attached by tenuous anchor-
lines of reference to the past and to the future, demands some chronological adjustment and an increased liberty of flight.

* * *

Retrospectively I am made aware of numerous
questions, completely evaded or attacked with an
over-elaborate feint of glancing blows. Gérard's
professionalism, his mechanical aptitude for writing
and that suspicious exuberance I have indefinitely
noticed? . . . There was more power and beauty,
Maurice de Guérin asserted, in the well-kept secret
of a man's self and his thoughts, than in the display

of a whole heaven he might have inside his breast,—
with this plausible summing-up, that the literary
career seemed to him unreal, both in its own essence
and in the rewards sought from it, hence "fatally
marred by a secret absurdity". How Guérin's precept,
favoured by an all-subduing devotional cast of mind,
affected his timid productivity, is sufficiently obvious,
and we must supplement it with the testimony of Baudelaire and Flaubert, writers who suffered and finally
subdued the same exquisite qualms of critical nausea.

A distaste for the vocation, for the mere business
of writing, may be coupled to the liveliest appreciation of the creator's potentialities. Draw a sharp
frontier, at which the province of the vocational
writer and the province of the "inspired", chance-
producing solitary slope together and converge.
Then what is Gérard's position? His earliest verses
—he was a precocious schoolboy—show the trace
of an unusually developed technical competence.
Patriotic and military themes. . . . He was sounding
an old trumpet his father, Surgeon-Major Labrunie,
had brought home from the Napoleonic campaigns,
entertaining a provincial and soon a much wider
audience, a nationalist poet of sixteen, and, when
he was twenty-two, hurling Cleon rhetoric against
the defunct Chamber of Deputies. But he translated
Goethe and won Goethe's written approval. Other
interests flourished, rank and wasteful. His uncle had

contributed vague pantheism, the amusements of folk-lore and archaeology, and a hoard of eighteenth-century Illuminist volumes. Gérard anomalously combined *solitary* and *virtuoso*, an agitated and difficult utterance inhabiting the labyrinthine corridors of an exceptional volubility. His instrument was capable of patriotic bass or journalist's crow; he precariously assembled the classical outlines of *Sylvie* from the dishevelled backs of envelopes and composed the dozen poems that ballast his reputation "*dans un état de rêverie supernaturaliste*".

From the subsequent years of disorder and purposeless travel, affected and involuntary eccentricities, nocturnal habits and so many projects unrealised, *Sylvie* emerged when Gérard was forty-five, —I must not say as justification, confusedly sentimentalising the indebtedness of an artist's work to his life,—but as explaining the mingled reticence and volubility which had jointly hampered him. It was *Octavie*, a much inferior story, Gérard sub-titled *L'Illusion*, and I suggest a provisional transference, —*Sylvie, ou l'Illusion. Sylvie* attuned the interval of calm, of creative assurance, which now interrupted a life mostly given up to storm and flux. . . . "J'ai saisi le fil d'Ariane, et dès lors toutes mes visions sont devenues célestes."—This thread had a remoter extension than he dreamed.

Built on a gently insurgent promontory, whence

it overlooks the backward prospect of unresting disappointments and delays, *Sylvie* resembles one of
those shrines of seaside Venus, slight counterparts
of Cnidian Aphrodite's citadel, which grateful trav-
ellers, the Anthology records, established here and
there along the shores of the Graeco-Roman world,
its materials themselves pathetically commemorat-
ing the artist's voyage, polished and whitened spars
of the wreck he had escaped, brittle flukes of weed
he had gathered, struggling inshore among the
treacherous crevices of the rocks, with empty shells,
stars of mica and, under an arch of formal scalloped
ornament, fluttering Venus, in act as though she
rode the calm, between clusters of dependent rib-
bon, wreaths of sand-poppy and crackling paper
streamers. Removed just beyond the sea's highest
wash, refuged in a coign of the broken tufa-cliff, the
voices of the element it has defied continually brim
this hollow like an ear, and a salt wind stiffens and
parches the drooping or blowing garlands,—appropriately, since the deity's office is both to prompt
and, afterwards, console. *Sylvie*, I mean, Gérard's
halcyon story, surmounted the conditions of its
origin but is still resonant with the echoes of that
emotional Chaos from whose bosom it has sprung.
Even the transparent felicity of its diction bespeaks a
hurly-burly momentarily eluded. Gérard, we know,
wrote against, as it were in spite of, the appalling press

and tangle of his ideas. "Je suis désolé", he once remarked, "me voilà aventuré dans une idée où je me
perds; je passe des heures entières à me retrouver.
... Croyez-vous que c'est à peine si je peux écrire
vingt lignes par jour, tant les ténèbres m'envahis-
sent!"—Enveloping shadows which threateningly
bound the lucid interspace.

Parenthetically I am obliged to admit my belief
that, with *Sylvie*, Gérard actually achieved what
Dumas had called *"un livre infaisable"*. "Je me suis
mis à traduire tous mes rêves, toutes mes émotions"
...; but, charged as it is with personal emphasis,
Sylvie treads a rhythmic, unhampered course. And I
reiterate that Gérard's work does not seem to me
important, as far as it irradiates or is the sentimental
consecration of his life: no, we are set about with
biographical detail, because a malady, call it, of his
art, so fused the personal and the artist self that
practically they are inseparable. *Everything which
lives is Holy* should be read oftener in an aesthetic
than in a mystical context, since, if all living things
appear worthy of the poet's rapture or scorn,
straightway he is lightened of an intolerable burden
of conflict: hatred and love do not require a gradual
assimilation but, unchallenged, glide towards the
centre: Skofield, no longer the aggressor from without, threads a phantasmal road among the smoky
flares of *Jerusalem*: and the lace-maker, the actress

79

and the nun, *Sylvie*, *Aurélia*, *Adrienne*, part the curdled evening vapours of Gérard's narrative.

I have suggested a borrowed sub-title—*L'Illusion*, but the word needs a preliminary cleansing of Romanticist associations. Gérard's fellowship with any group or any person was necessarily loose. The crowd-talent was foreign to his genius. He was an affectionate friend, yet a changeling humour either kept him apart, hidden, shifting rapidly through a series of bare lodgings, simultaneously rented, or brought him day by day to his friend's door, leading some maliciously chosen gift, a "serious, tranquil" lobster or a spotted Dalmatian, which he companioned during the next few days by a couple of smaller dogs. True, on the twenty-fifth of February, 1830, he had fought at the battle of *Hernani*, in the capacity of sergeant, and had been rewarded by Hugo, out of that special vein of absurdity which Baudelaire, an acridly observant critic of contemporary reputations, commented a quarter of a century later—("Je n'accepterais ni sa gloire, ni sa fortune, s'il me fallait en même temps *posséder* ses énormes ridicules")—with the pompous benediction: "Gérard, je suis content de vous!"

Fortuitous, then, as his acquaintanceship with the Romantics had been, Gérard differed from the company he kept in his attitude to the past and in the singularly tender and scrupulous use he made of tradition. Romanticism, surely, of every period and race, in this particular, has shown an ambiguous front. Romanticism has exploited and does still exploit the past—a great storehouse of frippery, a magazine of ancient halberds and corselets, pillaged and carried off, though the spoiler hardly understands their employment. And tradition has worn the immovable disdain of Racine's features, when they danced a derisive round before his bust in the *foyer* of the *Comédie Française*. A more equable, a humaner vision of the past seems alien to the Romantic temperament,—the past conceived of as a mistress, within whose embrace the young masculine heroism of the present dissolves its creative fatigue, a Phrygian goddess whose sons are also her lovers, waking only for the lover's return, whose "female will", like an indulgent mistress', stirs through profound and secret channels, seldom venturing a prohibition or an overt command.

Poussin's canvas, *Cephalus and Aurora*, where Cephalus strains against the goddess' reluctant arm, towards the winged horse, ready saddled and bitted, and the blessed Muses lie couched on their low hill, lapped in nocturnal vapours, warmed by the indistinguishable morning brightness of the sun-god's chariot, hurrying westward over the sea, may colour and strengthen the last image, besides exemplifying a Latin ability Gérard, too, possessed, of rehandling ancient materials with a skill, brusque, yet, all the while, apt and tender. Indeed, such a vision of the past is presupposed by a satisfactory orientation towards the future. Forecast, as well as retrospect, demands support of the historical method. And the various poets, whose achievement I have to review, none of them lacked that kind of sightless navel-string which, ideally, connects the writer and his epoch. Gérard made a notable anticipation of Verlaine's—

Je suis l'empire, à la fin de la décadence,

chancing upon this very same historical parallel, though many years earlier.

"Nous vivions alors", he wrote at the beginning of *Sylvie*, describing the years that witnessed his theatrical enslavement:

We were living at that time in one of those strange periods which usually follow a revolution or the downfall of some mighty empire. . . . It was composed of activity, diffidence and inertia, splendid utopian dreams, philosophic or religious aspirations, vague enthusiasms, the whole interpenetrated by certain instincts of renewal; the disagreeable impression of past troubles, fragile hopes—a period, may be, not unlike the period of Peregrinus and Apuleius. The earthy man yearned towards the bouquet of roses, held out to him by the beautiful hands of Isis, wherein he should find his regeneration. Eternally young and pure, the goddess appeared to us during sleep and put us to shame for the daylight hours we had wasted. *L'ambition n'était cependant pas de notre âge.* . . .

Let Gérard dress his own scene and qualify his own aspirations. He composed with this parallel in his mind,—that he was living in an age very similar to the age of Apuleius, with a kindred uneasiness and acute sense of transience, a kindred sense of that illusion which some monstrous political structure will germinate in its shadow, polypus city, breeding a phantom in each cell—

> Fourmillante cité, cité pleine de rêves,
> Où le spectre en plein jour raccroche le passant

—enfranchised, hence undirected, piety, here and there pricking a weak and startled head.

Political enthusiasms, in other periods a fruitful source of effort, were suffering a gradual eclipse. Gérard, Baudelaire, Villiers de l'Isle-Adam, Rimbaud, all committed themselves to waves of political excitement—Gérard in 1832, Baudelaire in 1848, Rimbaud during the Commune, Villiers hatching Legitimist plots—but found disenchantment and quickly absolved their attention. Penetrating indifference, traversed by violent flashes of factious revolutionary sentiment! "L'ambition n'était . . . pas de notre âge." And, while the social manifestations of that century of intellectual triumph and political ignominies continued to absorb their interest, fragmentarily and one by one they abandoned those careless hopes of political freedom which the rhetorical exhortations of the Romanticist leaders had speciously prompted.

And the ensuing emptiness must be lightened, rendered less deadly, by a severe application of oneself to oneself and a studious contemplation of one's own image reflected on the kindly flowing mirror of the past, whose mercy it is to ripple back only the few lineaments worth preservation, the shape of the brow and the cheeks and the cavernous darkness of the eyes. For they are our own sympathies and our own likeness which attract us into the past: but the journey is an expiation of vanities, trivalities, since it requires the expense of such concentration and such endeavour as are naturally least congenial to egotism. On that mirror of the past, Gérard and his self-selected Latin prototype were both ardent gazers. Unconcerned with naturalism, they enjoyed the sedulously cultivated "time-sense", to which Baudelaire referred in his essay, *Le Peintre de la vie moderne*, and which no writer who wishes his fancy to operate, be it even for a moment, outside the most obvious chronological restrictions, can afford safely to neglect. Thus, Gérard can be distinguished from Heine, with whose prose, I have suggested, *Sylvie* has a certain affinity. And, if Heine, in the *Romantic School*, criticises Novalis's *Heinrich von Ofterdingen* in terms of womanhood, of Sophia, the post-mistress' younger sister, near Göttingen, may we not, too, decry the prose-lyricism of *Reisebilder* and *Florentine Nights* as a German maiden, Bertha Lunken perhaps, whose sweet distant-look is, closer, belied by the prominent, pale-shining lobes of her skull, the fleshly protuberance of her lower lip, gleaming with a pensive fleck of saliva, and the rude cleft that an ugly recriminatory zeal sometimes scores between her eyes, with which it divides the rounded hillocks of her chin?

Heine's Gallicism, after all, could not dispel entirely the heavier national flavour. His workmanship, like the workmanship of a German draughtsman, had its crabbedness, its bugbear parades. We think of a northern fairy-story, the splintered pine-wood floor, the porcelain stove, and we think of the very words in which Heine attacked the creatures of his country-people's folk-imagination, comparing Melusina to a Teutonic elf and Morgan-la-Fay to a Brocken witch: the old woman with the prodigiously swollen stomach beats her drum, and the death-child, Mademoiselle Laurence, bends low near the ground, listening to her mother's knock against the damp lid of her coffin,—or else, "the wild swan spreads its wings" and flies away, north, south, east or west, who cares whither?

*   *   *

Take away the showered-down accumulation of

Gérard's fancy, and you uncover a hollow human cast, whose measurements an examination of ancient play-bills or the articles of forgotten dramatic-critics might equally well have served to establish. They are the measurements of an actress of the second or third order, called Jenny Colon, by Gérard called *Aurélia*, half actress and half demi-mondaine, the legitimate descendant of those *figurantes* who, in Casanova's day, received no salary, and who, it was even once debated, might fairly be expected to pay a small rent for the advantageous position their commerce occupied under the brightly lit arcades of scenic illusion. All that was terrestrial of this phantom, its place in time, its real ambitions and inclinations mattered to Gérard quite as little as it need delay us. ". . . La femme réelle révoltait notre ingénuité." The identifications of a belovèd, a desired object with the response it wakens, is a Romanticist foible: qualities lent by the worshipper, against which the object of his cult may perhaps be seen feebly struggling, tentatively disengaging his or her naked limbs from the ceremonial costume in which they have been ignorantly sheathed, are presumed inherent, as though devotion only held a lamp.

The literary output of the nineteenth century shows us triumphant feminism, Romantic in its origin but rapidly vulgarised, and its contradiction, the bile-black misogyny of Nietzsche and Strindberg. Further and further retiring into the Vatican of her clothes, more and more flagrantly emphasising the sanctity of her favours by the impregnable consequence with which she surrounded them, every pin and every bow and every *ruche* a Papal guard, Vala saw her rising credit touch an unprecedented height. But the reaction concerns us, as far as it was expressed in the new specialised manner of feeling Gérard initiated. To be irresistible, he was aware, an attraction must be inexplicable as well. "Nous aimons les femmes", Baudelaire wrote, "à proportion qu'elles nous sont plus étrangères. Aimer les femmes intelligentes est un plaisir de pédéraste." Where an attraction is reasoned, there may it be assaulted and there its dominant power will, first of all, decline. And, to remain permanent, this attraction must remain unfulfilled. "Posséder, c'est n'y plus penser; mais perdre, c'est posséder indéfiniment en esprit". So Gérard, when he learned that some abrupt mutation of the *Bourse* had repaired his crumbling fortunes almost in a night, dismissed from his mind any thought of possible conquest. He would not supplant Aurélia's titular lover,—a young man at the card-table, pale-faced, nervous, his eyes of melancholy sweetness, throwing down his stakes and immediately losing them with an air of complete indifference. For, like Marcel Proust, who, in the general acuteness of his observatory faculties, as conspicuously out-measures Gérard as his prolonged retrospective journey outstripped Gérard's midnight drive towards Ermenonville and the past, he made a novel distinction between the object and the response it stirs, a response of which the swelling and dying vibrations may be enjoyed, though the object is contemptible or, perhaps, beckons us far beyond reach.

Thus he affected the stage and its populace—poor caryatids, whose whitened brows upbear such a massive architrave of illusion. And, night after night, he watched the same repeated miracle. A spirit, already formidably armed by reading and travel, deployed its combined forces around an object, whose palpable vulgarity only whipped his pleasures, just as the intrusion of a personal curiosity might emphasise the impersonal beauty of the whole. "Quelle est donc cette comédienne? . . . Est-elle bien aussi jeune, aussi fraîche, aussi honnête qu'elle le paraît? Sont-ce de vraies perles et de fines opales qui ruissellent parmi ses blonds cheveux cendrés, et ce voile de dentelle appartient-il bien légitimement à cette malheureuse enfant?"

Dandyism crept in, the dandyism of his epoch. Gautier, the *Journal* of the Goncourts reports, as well as Gavarni and others, severally looked back to the 'thirties with regret, with lingering affection. They were years in an obvious contrast to the Second Empire, years of which a generous extravagance was the characteristic, when delights were simpler, more naïve, when young men, Gavarni himself for example, loved virtuous and mature *bourgeoises*, often without hope of return, spent the fine weather among white dresses upon the deep grass of the river-bank, passed much of the night in endless and exalted conversation. Then, "le beau ténébreux" was fashionable. And while the woman's skirt kept imperceptibly expanding—Is it not a pity that the cinematograph, which condenses the expansion of living petals into the compass of some minutes, cannot, synthetically, represent the unfolding, flowering, decadence of a mode, with the minor, exquisite coruscation of combs, brooches, ribbons, lace?—masculine arbiters permitted a certain carelessness, a certain exuberance and languor, about the linen, the hair, the coverings of the neck, to alternate with a cut otherwise rigorous, *serré*, and of rather military style.

Gérard inoculated his story with this toxin of sentiment, "dating" his work, yet also magnifying its chances of survival. As a conscious smile betrays the sleeper, an idiosyncracy, which it would have been hard for him to control, showed luminous through the topical disguise. I have mentioned his indebtedness to the theatre. Like Degas, who devised a transparency, where the theatre and its people, their squalor, fictitious splendour, the striking and

pathetic antitheses their life affords, are seen metamorphosed, behind a thin, unwrinkled glaze, or like
Constantin Guys, whose sombre ground encloses
some kept-woman, a woman of the highest circles of
the demi-monde, crossed knees and impudently lifted
petticoats, the *lorette* or the *pierreuse*, the "street-
walker", her hands thrust defiantly into the two
pockets of a voluminous black apron, each figure
emerging with a sublimity that seems to concentrate
and underline all the features of her trade, Gérard
would portray a given circumstance with the skill
that omits temporal distractions, yet never invali-
dates its actuality. The dancer's thudding feet are
noiseless. As in Degas's picture, the painted back-
cloth has been rolled up out of sight and a wider
prospect is discovered: a wave breaks silently, mar-
bling the humid sand. Gérard interpolated phrases,
imagery, startling though not displeasing in their
context, so sonorous that their effect brims the suc-
ceeding page. And if he enters a convent parlour,
where the novices are performing a mystery-play, he
does not watch some insipid religious farce; no—

Ce que je vis jouer était comme un mystère des anciens
temps. Les costumes, composés de longues robes, n'étaient
variés que par les couleurs de l'azur, de l'hyacinthe ou de
l'aurore. La scène se passait entre les anges, sur les débris du
monde détruit. . . .

The result—happy amalgamation of genius and

THE STREET-WALKER: Drawing by Constantin Guys

hazard, for *Sylvie*, with every other work of high aesthetic attainment, insists that, after all, human ingenuity may do no more than shed its seed in the creative lap of chance—appears, now and again, as having reached its effects by a method of which, I think, "harmonic" might be, perhaps, the best qualification. A primary theme introduced, the theme of *Aurélia*, the lighted stage, the descending curtain, her lover glanced at near the card-table, "l'amère tristesse que laisse un songe évanoui", Gérard set eyes upon the advertisement of a provincial fête,— *Sylvie* must be dancing there,—and drove away towards the past;—another and opposing theme, simple, yet artfully complicated by the traditional melodies of the Valois—

> La belle était assise
> Près du ruisseau coulant,
> Et dans l'eau qui frétille,
> Baignait ses pieds blancs. . . .

—till it has reached its culmination, *Adrienne's* song among the listening group of peasant children.

In counterpoint, returns the memory of *Aurélia*. But with a sudden, daring legerdemain which falsifies expectation, Gérard has reconciled the combatants: "C'étaient les deux moitiés d'un seul amour", and, much as the satisfaction of urgent physical desire, however brutal, will lend the pupils an unaccustomed, vaporous glow, smooth the puckered brow

and cheeks and ennoble the taut and anxious structure of the body, thereafter the narrative recedes en-
nobled, on that very gradual decline which classical
examples have taught us to prefer. "J'ai saisi le fil
d'Ariane", and this, no doubt, was Ariadne's clue.
The spectacle of impermanence may provide a more
lasting comfort than any prospect of eternal well-
being and the "intermittences of the heart" a keener
enjoyment than any static paradise. So—

 . . . Lente, lente currite, noctis equi!

Yes, slowly, slowly, but do not stop, or the pleasure
you are dragging with you would vanish as it ceased
to move away! Both Gérard and Proust spun their
thread-like system of aesthetic correspondences over
the warring themes of an emotional chaos. One face
conceals another, one transitory grace reveals its
fellow. The writer's sensibility stands unmoved,
always maintaining its central authority, just as the
dreamer protests his real corporeal presence against
the whirlwind of his self-concerted torments.

 Comparatively, *Le Rêve et la Vie* is the matrix of
confusion, from which *Sylvie* has been drawn. The
writer's cloudy preoccupations had grown so vast,
so overweening that the narrow chambers of art
proved scarcely ample enough to house them. They
demanded the license of a strictly autobiographical
form, and Gérard began the chronicle of his delu-

sions, writing painfully, yet with the sort of cold impetuosity and low-pitched vehemence that breathes
in the voice of a somnambulist. "Quelque jour
j'écrirai l'histoire de cette 'descente aux enfers'." . . .
And now he had fulfilled his promise. He related his
hallucinations, manias, the follies into which he was
not seldom led, embroiling his recital with passages,
of which the clear and heavy note reminds us that he
was fast losing control of the machinery of expression, not losing the gift itself:—how, immured in a
suburban Bedlam, he came to believe that the other
lunatics, caught sight of in the garden-walks, had
each some different influence upon the celestial
bodies: an old man, busily tying knots, while he
consulted his watch, was charged with the progress
of the hours: to another, assiduously pacing out a
crazy circle, belonged the daily itinerary of the Sun:
the regulation of the Moon was Gérard's own duty.
Certainly, his natural eloquence was still alive, and
the attitude of the narrator, sedulously objective,
kept his story innocent of tedium. The visionary
seems to have hardly resented the straight-jacket and
the douche. He could detail the catalogue of his
sufferings, and never forfeit the supreme decorum of
art:

   . . . J'ai deux fois vainqueur traversé l'Achéron.

With an impersonal and dignified gesture, he could
point to their supposed origin,—his books heaped

along the wall, "la Tour de Babel en deux cent tomes",—they alone were enough to send a sane man raving mad!—or exclaim: "Aimer une religieuse sous la forme d'une actrice! . . . et si c'était la même! Il y a de quoi devenir fou!"

But *Le Rêve et la Vie* was interrupted [1] by Gérard's death. He had been found hanging, attached to the rusty window-bar of a tramps' lodging-house that, sometime earlier in the morning, some hours before dawn, had refused him entrance. It was mid-winter and a season exceptionally cruel. Gérard had no overcoat. The event made a little stir, and next day there drove up Anna Deslions, then approaching the imperial noon-tide of her reputation, and several high-priced courtesans, all crowded under the hood of a *fiacre*. Anna Deslions climbed down and touched the iron bar with her fingers: might it bring her luck! Concealed about the dead man's clothes was an additional scrap of manuscript, twined with copious marginalia — kabbalistic scrawlings and the doctrine of the Immaculate Conception, demonstrated by geometrical argument. *La Suite manque*—and that is a verdict which might be written

---

[1] M. Pierre Audiat has devoted a first chapter of his interesting little book—(*L'Aurélia de Gérard de Nerval,* 1926)—to a history of the successive stages through which *Aurélia* passed. The undertaking, he suggests, was virtually complete on Gérard's death, but wanted revision; that Gérard had ever purposed a third part is a misconception, fostered by Gautier's prefatory note, in the edition of 1855.

across the entire field of Gérard's literary achievement. Yet justice is bound to admit that his shortcomings are rather those of a perplexed affluence than such faults as generally stigmatise the pretensions of a teased sterility. And, if *Sylvie* marked the formal victory of his prose, his verse had already signalised its conquest,—performance equally slight in volume but of no less permanent and unmistakable reveberation.

He was already the author of *Les Cydalises*:

> Où sont nos amoureuses?
> Elles sont au tombeau! . . .

and, between 1843 and 1845, had written *Le Christ aux Oliviers*, *Vers dorés* and the sonnet named *Delfica*. From the pretty landscape verse of *La Cousine*, chiefly remarkable for the skill which has compelled this infinitesimal grain to produce even so small a verdant shoot—

> L'hiver a ses plaisirs: et souvent, le dimanche,
> Quand un peu de soleil jaunit la terre blanche,
> Avec une cousine on sort se promener . . .
> "Et ne vous faites pas attendre pour dîner,"
> Dit la mère.
>   Et, quand on a bien, aux Tuileries,
> Vu sous les arbres noirs les toilettes fleuries,
> La jeune fille a froid . . . et vous fait observer
> Que le brouillard de soir commence à se lever.

—he had advanced, and, through the latter twelve

years of his life was still constantly advancing towards a method of expression which should omit nothing of his potentiality, which should include his capacity for direct and moving statement, for veiled, allusive reference; which should combine religious faith,—his innocuous charlatanism and its resounding abracadabra, the deceptive enjoyments of which he shared with Blake,—as well as the pronounced scepticism that tempered his religiosity. *Vers dorés* and the slow, passionate emphasis of its measure, abrupt, brief sentences projected like separate, momentous shafts—

> Crains, dans le mur aveugle, un regard qui t'épie:
> A la matière même un verbe est attaché . . .
> Ne la fais pas servir à quelque usage impie!

> Souvent dans l'être obscur habite un dieu caché;
> Et, comme un œil naissant couvert par ses paupières,
> Un pur esprit s'accroît sous l'écorce de pierres!

—does not mark the limit of his attempt. *El Desdichado*, written in 1853, has gained by a sort of flexibility, and round this poem Gérard's commentator can do no better than marshal his previous annotations, since the daring plan comprehends a far wider range of sound and imagery than he can hope to analyse piecemeal,—a poem I must ask leave to transcribe in full, each line resembling the "first line" of a musical composition,—as though each line

might be the provocation of another poem or sequence of poems,—yet the whole composition being
indivisibly knit:

> Je suis le ténébreux,—le veuf,—l'inconsolé,
> Le prince d'Aquitaine à la tour abolie:
> Ma seule *étoile* est morte,—et mon luth constellé
> Porte le *soleil noir* de la *Mélancolie.*
>
> Dans la nuit du tombeau, toi qui m'as consolé,
> Rends-moi le Pausilippe et la mer d'Italie,
> La *fleur* qui plaisait tant à mon cœur désolé,
> Et la treille où le pampre à la rose s'allie.
>
> Suis-je Amour ou Phébus, Lusignan ou Biron?
> Mon front est rouge encore du baiser de la reine;
> J'ai rêvé dans la grotte où nage la sirène. . . .
>
> Et j'ai deux fois vainqueur traversé l'Achéron:
> Modulant tour à tour sur la lyre d'Orphée
> Les soupirs de la sainte et les cris de la fée.

*   *   *

Now, of all the poets we are agreed to call *Symbolist*, Gérard was, I think, the most imperfect and
his success the most accidental. But, so long unused,
his poetic instrument is, for that, none the less worth
admiration and his studied "modulations" strike no
less delightfully upon an ear so tuned by verse that
it will catch responsive echoes from the past and
from the future. Perhaps they are unique. Yet, supposing the anonymous authorship of *El Desdichado*

were in question, we might do more unwisely than suggest the poet of *Les Correspondances*. Confronted by such obvious dissimilarities, I have been loth to stretch an analogy between Gérard de Nerval and Baudelaire,—of whose sonnet Gérard's distracted career among a "forest of symbols" had proved much too literally the anticipation and the astounding type.

VILLIERS DE L'ISLE-ADAM

THERE are some writers whose contribution to our sensibility is fluid;—of these, among the foremost I should place Gérard de Nerval;—and others there are whose achievement by opposition might be called *statuary*, so definite is the contribution they bring, as though they had gone to the trouble of refurnishing a part of our minds with material, solid and brilliantly palpable objects.

The genius of Villiers de l'Isle-Adam, though it must have expired amid that haze of apparent failure which is the necessary concomitant and penalty of all wide-flung plans and inordinate ambitions, though its scene was laid amid such disorder and under conditions of such misfortune as Gérard himself even can hardly have experienced, will provide its student with a range of pleasures singularly distinct and concrete. From writers of the category to which Gérard de Nerval belongs, a reader comes away, his senses quickened and subtilised: the extent of his hearing, he believes, has been increased: his mind has received an addition, permanent yet indefinable and fluid. Comparatively, how sharp is the impact of Villiers' prose! The auditory scope has been enlarged by practical demonstration, and those new provinces of enjoyment are already occupied by the forces of an unknown and disturbing melody. Here, as it so often happens, the components of personal failure had also proved the components of aesthetic success. Here again was at work that interior economy to which I have previously referred. Nothing or almost nothing of Villiers' idiosyncrasies but could find its proper place and function in his growth—Royalism, Clericalism and the peculiar defiance of his own narrative method rearing their luckless heads against Republicanism, Agnosticism and the then fashionable tendencies of current literature. As if to make this assembly of prejudice more dangerous and more probably fatal, it was complicated by the immense and absorbing pride of his name and lineage.

So homogeneous, indeed, is the effect of Villiers' art that I shall be at a loss to give a more detailed account of its beauties, except after first attempting to infuse something of its colour and prevailing climate. Retrograde as he will appear from the characteristics I have noted above, many of Villiers' sources, while he composed, lay in the immediate past. He had been born in the reign of Louis-Philippe; his maturity saw the Second Empire and the Third Republic, but it is to the annals of an earlier generation, to the earlier decades of the nineteenth century that a critic of Villiers' work must chiefly turn for enlightenment. Now, there are cer-

tain phases of the past, which, though distantly we
may apprehend their configuration and general tenor,
we can never hope to bring into any near relation
with our contemporary problems. No period, I suppose, of modern literature is at present further removed from our understanding than the first fifty
years of the nineteenth century; its protagonists continue mysterious as long as they survive. Berlioz—
what a remote figure his *Memoirs* reveal, how ex-
ultantly carried away by maelstroms of passion,
those snowy nights he spent in a ploughed field, the
exhausting vivacity of his spirit! The daemonic
energies of these men are like voiceless cyclones: we
notice the havoc they have made and watch the
forest bend and break, the water crowding before
them in angry hillocks and ridges; but we cannot
hear the accompanying tumult and we cannot tell
whence it blows,—a Romantic storm-piece still in
motion, still writhing and soughing. We must be
content, then, with an approximate representation,
and I resort to Danhauser's picture, *Liszt at the
Piano*, where, appropriately enough, behind Beet-
hoven's colossal marble effigy, a veritable storm has
empurpled the horizon, seen through a wide-opened
casement. Madame Sand twists sideways in her chair
and with one hand checks her busy amanuensis. The
Comtesse d'Agoult leans her brow against the ex-
tremity of the key-board. Berlioz is tender and pen-

sive, while, in the background, Rossini has flung his arm round Paganini's shoulders, Paganini standing there upright and inky black, the face of the Sabbatic Goat gazing out from between the wide white wings of his collar. That canvas was painted in 1840, eight years, that is to say, before the Romantic Movement reached what ought perhaps to be considered as its proper climax, 1848, the year of terror and revolution. Similarly, it is in the drawings of Gavarni and Devéria that we shall find the minor lyricism of the period most conveniently epitomised. Tagged, frilled and puffed, the creations Gavarni illustrated for the pages of *La Mode*, and the young wearers who set them off, with their coiffures drawn so elaborately under the comb and the rather inconsequent lightness of their flying carriage,—Gavarni's fashion-plates alone show sufficient trace of the prevailing sensibility. Let us admire, too, his lithographed representations of public balls and masquerades, and an engraving by Noel after Gavarni, called *The Walk*;—it breathes such a penetrating aroma of autumnal confidences, across the stubble, down hollow lanes soft underfoot with the accumulation of dead leaves, of resolutions, promises to write:

> Rien de bruyant, rien d'agité
> Dans leur triste félicité!

And, once again, it presents us with an apparition of

le beau ténébreux, the disconsolate *Enfant du Siècle*, his large, swimming eyes, his scarcely perceptible moustache and beard, his exuberant *chevelure*, as he paces arm-in-arm with his companion, the points of his cravat and the full skirts of his coat agitated at the caprice of a vagrant wind.

And this manner of feeling, I suggest, either tempestuous and headlong or cadenced and exquisitely poignant, was to Villiers more sympathetic and more valuable than any of which latter-day moods gave him the choice. "*Le beau ténébreux*" it was natural he should prefer, granted his temperament and upbringing, when the shadowy hero had been succeeded in the drawing-rooms of Paris, as Edmond de Goncourt remarked, by an amalgam of cynical poise and unamiable buffoonery. The Second Empire was a period which alike depressed and intensely stimulated its main actors. Along its parade-ground and its gas-lit boulevard, irradiated here and there by the cuirass of an Imperial guard nan, the "mahogany-shining" flanks of his mount, by the "dazzling equipage" of a Cora Pearl or a Hortense Schneider, eight-springed and thickly upholstered, Villiers' progress was enveloped in a certain cool, protective cloud of antiquated sentiment. Though traversing a world, say, of which the line, the line of its furniture, the line of its clothes, grew increasingly billowy and squab, his brain preserved the memory of simpler perpendicular folds, thin silks and cashmeres dropping almost straight from the shoulder's boss to the narrow spring of the ankle, while here were velvets and other rich, substantial stuffs swelling horizontally from the waist, heavy with reduplicate flounces, as if upon the imagined amplitude of the hips too startling an emphasis could never be set. Villiers' method demanded the escarpments and abrupt sallies of emotion. He beckoned the chimaeras of Romantic sentiment, now diffident and grown slightly timid; this reactionary gesture was almost half ironic.

Irony—we must dismiss the word should it do no better than evoke that sad, hesitant mixture of alarm and exasperation with which we answer threats and cure the sting of blows. Yet an element, of which "irony" is the readiest designation, did in fact serve Villiers' purpose, anchoring to the terms of our common experience the flight of daemonic personages, otherwise preposterous or quite intractable. Thus he so decreased the pressure of an atmosphere intolerably rarefied, till it could accommodate ordinary requirements—thus obeying, as in all else, the exigences of his narrative scheme. But, as often as we speak of Villiers as a story-teller, as a master of narrative art, we must make the ensuing reservation,— that neither in the development of the narrative itself nor in the development of character lay his chief interest; that he was primarily concerned with the emotions of his personages, to the nearly complete exclusion of their strictly personal significance; that he was chary of detail as the naturalist is greedy; that, while the naturalist laboured to fix his creatures within exact limits of time and space, Villiers would have regarded as insufferable any such restraint. His stories reflect the *colour* of an emotion; they do not reproduce or make any attempt to reproduce the irregular *shape* imposed by circumstance. Let us exclude temporal irregularities, and transport our theme to a world fabulous or closely neighbouring the fabulous, not idealised, of course, but the very same world which the conventions of classical drama afford, where potentialities of feeling, rather than feelings themselves, the refinement of jealousy and the extremes of love, have an unencumbered scope and every emotion can release its full capacity of brilliance. The incompleteness of a situation was the naturalist's concern; its realisation belonged to Villiers. Consistency distinguished his method. As a story-teller he postulated a set of conditions, then logically fulfilled them. His characters are "unreal" in the naturalist's sense, less by token of the almost invariable distinction of their *tenue* and the innocent sumptuousness of their environment, than because, given a set of conditions, they always behave with a kind of exalted consistency. They are true to themselves, hence unreal to a realist and real to a poet;

they are as phantasmal and as essential as Milton's *Arch-Fiend* and *Samson*.

Before venturing further it may be well to deal briefly with the verbal medium through which these qualities were expressed; but I am obliged to add that the cleavage presupposed may convey, perhaps, hardly a just estimate of the style whose particular grace it was to allow a fissure so very small betwixt the manner and the subject, the design and the execution, which has, besides, a supernumerary grace specially comforting to modern ears. A student of weekly reviews, for example, of the great mass of modern fiction, becomes accustomed to the flat and even tenor of such prose, composed and written down, it would seem in print, as though the writer had put away his pen and taken up the compositor's stick instead. Temporarily deadened, his ear recaptures with delight the exquisite familiarity of the human voice: not, it is true, our habitual speech, our abrupt unfinished sentences, rambling tautological inversions and endless repetition, but still the human voice, as it might well but may never proceed from our lips, purified and dilated by emotion, yet conserving the essential character of speech,—mediating between a silent, formless world and another world of inarticulate clamour and bustle, like the cool and resonant hour which divides the day and the night. So animate, though extremely indirect and allusive, is Villiers' prose. His word-sensitiveness he maintained intact against the quotidian stress of journalism, and he wrote carefully, altering one in every five words, murmuring over what he had written, more°audibly then, and, at last, in the solitude of his chamber, rehearsing it aloud in bold and melodious accents.

Pausing, I must insist that Villiers' diction was not the "phrase parlée", the sort of conversational easiness which Marcel Proust attacked in the second of his two concluding volumes: ". . . le petit sourire, la petite grimace, qui altère à tout moment . . . la phrase parlée de Sainte-Beuve"; though parenthetically it is amusing to notice that M. Jean Cocteau's posthumous tribute credits Proust's style with exactly those same reprehensible characteristics: "Il m'est difficile de *lire* son œuvre", he writes, "au lieu de l'*entendre*", since through every chapter he visualises the novelist's smile, shrug, gloves, moustaches. . . . Similarly throughout Villiers' prose we hear a voice and, with the help of their printed equivalent starring, italicising the page, interposing the abrupt solemnity of a row of capitals, we envisage the accompaniment of his precise yet abundant gestures. A voice we hear; but it is not a voice easy or bland, not the voice of a writer of weekly *causeries*. A needless precaution it was, if he exhausted every variety of the typographer's art, deliberately so as to distinguish his method; his stories are all of them written *aloud*. And he was best suited when the story could be delivered, as *Tribulat Bonhomet* is delivered, in a kind of oration or discourse, this device permitting the narrator to wheel about more rapidly, more speciously introduce his digressions, dismiss and re-call his personages with the minimum of labour.

Such are the marks of his constant effort towards suppleness,—a pianist practising his fingers-stretch upon the keys. We forget so ruthlessly, he may have thought, and we forget so rapidly—human minds, even the commonest of them, running heavy with half-obliterated pains and enjoyments that they will presently slough off and lose. Then, if the move-ment called Symbolism is of account at all, it should include elements equally foreign to the redundancy of the Romantic revival and to the prohibitive severity of Classicism; it must be catholic (as, in another sense, Villiers was Catholic) and comprehend always wider and finer shades of emotion, *nuances* hitherto uncharted and unrecorded,—an aim shared by the different writers whom he preceded, its violent and irritative effect upon Rimbaud, for example, making of him a kind of megalomaniac adventurer, its more placid and leisurely working upon the genius of Mallarmé investing him with the consequence of arch-priest: poor Rimbaud, driven out by his formal preoccupations into the desert of not-being and chaos; poor Mallarmé, the glassy limits of his shrine yearly closing around him! Less elaborately equipped, then how should Villiers succeed? And it was perhaps a certain singleness of intelligence which came most readily to his support. He was Catholic, we remember, and Legitimist; the implied restrictions provided a necessary clog. So overwhelmingly prolific is our modern life, so bewildering are the possibilities it suggests! So disheartening is our habitual lack of bias! Fortunate nowadays is the writer who possesses a temperament naturally selective. The strict choice of his material must not be confounded with narrowness. Villiers' antecedents played a part, as I shall try to show, and the part they played was beneficial. "Le Catholicisme", another Catholic writer, Barbey d'Aurevilly, had declared, "est la science du bien et du mal. . . . Soyons mâles, larges, opulents comme la vérité éternelle." A dogma is of value merely if it can instil a conviction as absolute as that! So on the discouraging spectacle a light was concentrated which might claim, and did at least aspire, to be as impartial, fiercely lucid, as full and as masculine as the arc-light of eternal verity. Into this beam—is it not understandable that the sheer intensity of its glow should accomplish a relentless modification of individual traits?—sprang a multiplicity of images, diverse, yet none of them utterly dissimilar. Presented in frank, radiant planes, like the figures Manet painted, they assume the order of their recession and prominence. Some stand out salient and hard; of others the rudimentary outline is allowed to appear:

Accoudée auprès d'un candélabre, la reine Victoria s'était attardée, ce soir-là, en audience extraordinaire. A côté d'elle, sur un tabouret d'ivoire, était assise une jeune liseuse, miss Héléna H. . . .

—an impression as effaced and as pure as the profile of a worn Victorian halfpenny!

A reminiscence, too, of *Keepsake* beauties, you observe,—wreathed English pansies and wanton German forget-me-nots! The young reader on her ivory-legged stool, swan-stuffed and covered, no doubt, in tartan or *grenat* coloured silk, is the be-trothed of the *Duke of Portland*, last seen crossing Hyde Park at night, his armorial carriage surrounded by a galloping cavalcade of torch-bearing outriders. He has brought back leprosy from the East; hence the dreadful consequence which surrounds his move-ments. Villiers' story of the pair of lovers so radically unfortunate is much inferior to his best, and I have selected it because the fulgurant apparition of the Duke of Portland's carriage, when it first traversed my mind, torch-light flaring across its varnished panels, amid the shadowy embroidery of horses' legs, recalled a drawing by Constantin Guys, or rather the generalised recollection of several drawings. Here was a similarity which might be expanded to some purpose. Returning from his Eastern travels, Guys brought home—not leprosy, but a kind of freshness, strangeness towards the usages of his own people. His drawings, whether they are drawings of the demi-monde, of the interior of a soldier's brothel, of a ball, a review, or of a carriage rolling down a sandy avenue of the Bois behind two high-stepping, brittle-shanked bays, reflect that gleam of Romantic surprise and interest which was predominant in the beholder. A fountain-head of pleasurable amazement, never dried up so long as the artist maintained his isolation and contemplative reserve! To Villiers I should attribute a kindred strangeness, the same fruitful bewilderment; but we must make this supplementary note,—that if Villiers, as indeed it so frequently happened, laid his scene among surroundings of such transcendent magnificence that the preliminary catalogue of their splendours has the effect of some sonorous orchestral overture, he was looking backwards from without, from poverty and neglect, upon an illusory world, of which, or so he believed, his birth should have given him the freedom. "Moi ... le prince ignoré ... le désherité ... le banni de liesse!" And his complaint was further aggravated by the addition of spiritual pride:

Je sens, alors, que je porte dans mon âme le reflet des richesses stériles d'un grand nombre de rois oubliés.

While, elsewhere:

Que nous importe la justice (he wrote)? Celui qui en naissant ne porte pas dans sa poitrine sa propre gloire ne connaîtra jamais la signification réelle de ce mot.

"Ces paroles", Verlaine commented in *Les Poètes maudits*, "donnent tout Villiers de l'Isle-Adam, l'homme et l'œuvre—orgueil immense, justifié"—within its limits a perfectly just criticism, but which may set us musing that a writer for whom it was impossible to place the smallest degree of confidence on the judgement of his fellows would find an intolerable strain devolving on himself; "the Areopagy and dark Tribunal" of his thoughts, sitting behind closed doors, would become a focus of distress, the tyrannous, embittered senate of a circumscribed realm; sullenness, perhaps would result, or lethargy, —at best, a conscious and mannered gait, a defensive stiffness, displayed alike by his personages and their creator.

* * . *

Like their creator, each bearing with him the conscious burden of his interior glory or, it may be, of his shame, a little rigid and aloof in consequence, of gestures nervous and a little abrupt, Villiers' personages occupy a curious midway position between the individual and the general, between figures which are principally abstractions and figures which are chiefly portraits. As though he had deliberately made his way backwards down the grade of pictorial and narrative development, halting just at that point where the Koré's subtle individual smile begins to irradiate the stylised lineaments of her type, where the resonance of the hero's name, *Odysseus* say, begins to mingle with the renown of his attributes, guile, ruthlessness, and fuse in a single living personality, the story-teller's craft enabled the creatures of his imagination to resume each the impersonal splendour of its attributes,—a polychrome range of statuary, *Beauty* with its tender eye-purple, *Heroism* with its masculine nimbus of fiery rays, much as a painter troubled to retain some shreds and trappings of her divinity round the coarse, salient womanhood of his Tuscan, Venetian, or Flemish model. For in the pomegranate, the traditional curve of the arm enclosing her naked or swaddled offspring, in the hand which dips a pen to write her *Magnificat*, in her aureole and angelic attendants, divinity reposes, while Realism coaxed the texture of Virgin's brow, lips, cheek into sharper and more human prominence. Against the rapid, destructive progress of mechanical skill every artist must now and then formulate his protest, opposing the entire weight of his genius. And thus Villiers did, immensely simplifying his creation, confident that once a territory has undergone strict survey and enclosure, thereby the enchanting variety of the ground is only a thousand times increased.

And what variety, what fine gradations! From the mass of conjectures hazarded above I should like to deduce a hypothetical architecture of Villiers' talent, capacious enough, rooms, cells, and pavilions, to include this diverse assembly of creatures. Such pains the creator himself spent housing them! But that consideration brings us directly to another,— the dexterity, I mean, with which Villiers composed his exordium, the singular aptitude with which out of the tangled materials of his story he plucked the first tenuous inch of narrative thread. "Celui . . . qui veut écrire son rêve se doit d'être infiniment éveillé" . . . and here there was allowable no false start, clumsy reeling off of several parallel strands afterwards knotted together; the rhythm of the opening sentences attunes our expectancy and preludes the elaboration of the theme. A Romanticist theme Villiers usually chose, one reminiscent very often of those extravagantly exalted serials, in which, as early as 1830 and in the pages of *La Mode* and other journals of a similar kind, Villiers' mannerisms were being clumsily anticipated: [1]

Lord Edwin Sydnam venait de perdre sa mère; dans son désespoir, il semblait sur le point de succomber lui-même à cette maladie si bien nommée *brochen heart*; à cette langueur

---

[1] From "Le Majordome": *La Mode*, 1830.

mortelle que l'amour filial disputait à l'autre amour pour la première fois.

Orphelin à vingt ans, possesseur d'une fortune considérable, appelé par son rang, par ses talents distingués aux plus honorables emplois, Edwin languissait depuis six mois dans une sombre mélancholie, lorsqu'un des camarades vint le visiter dans son château d'Erington. . . .

We accept Villiers' romanticism as we should accept the preference of a composer for an earlier, more naïve musical idiom. In this context, I remember Jules Laforgue; yet a difference is apparent as soon as you come to scrutinise their respective peculiarities,—Laforgue's rather deliberate approach, his anxiety to reawaken the dormant blossoms of superannuated sentiment and, through nostrils ironically dilated, to inhale a large waft of forgotten sweetness:

Ah! que tout n'est-il opéra-comique! . . . Que tout n'évolue-t-il en mesure sur cette valse anglaise *Myosotis*, qu'on entendait cette année-là (moi, navré, dans les coins, comme on pense) au Casino, valse si décemment mélancolique, si irréparablement derniers, derniers beaux jours! . . . (Cette valse, oh! si je pouvais vous en inoculer d'un mot le sentiment avant de vous laisser entrer en cette histoire!)

—making a contrast as obvious to Villiers' manner of "inoculation" as do the lines I have transcribed below, from his story called *Conte de fin d'été*:

En province, au tomber du crépuscule sur les petites villes, —vers les six heures, par exemple, aux approches de l'automne,—il semble que les citadins cherchent de leur mieux à s'isoler de l'imminente gravité du soir: chacun rentre en son coquillage au pressentiment de tout ce danger d'étoiles qui pourrait induire à "penser".—Aussi, le singulier silence, qui se produit alors, paraît-il émaner, en partie, de l'atonie compassée des figures sur les seuils. C'est l'heure où l'écrasis criard des charrettes va s'éteignant du côté des routes.—A présent, aux promenades,—"cours des *Belles-Manières*"—bruit, plus distinctement, par les airs, sur l'isolement des quinconces, le frisson triste des hautes feuillées. Au long des rues s'enchangent, entre ombres, des saluts rapides. . . . Et, des reflets ternes de la brune sur les pierres et les vitres, de l'impression nulle et morne dont l'espace est pénétré—se dégage une si poignante sensation de vide, que l'on se croirait chez des défunts . . .

to the opening paragraphs (longer than I can interpolate here) of *Un Dîner d'athées*, for example, in Barbey d'Aurevilly's *Diaboliques*.

But *Un Dîner d'athées*, the profusion of horror which it lets loose, the Delacroix violence of its rhythms, will serve to distinguish Villiers' method from that of Barbey d'Aurevilly, just as surely as, viewed from the standpoint of Jules Laforgue, his virtuosity and deliberately exploited sentiment, those twin eminences might seem to be close neighbours. Both cultivated the immoderate. "Je ne suis pas tendre, je suis excessif", *un enfant du siècle* had declared. "Hélas, vois-tu bien", Villiers might have replied in *Maryelle's* phrase, "nul n'est plus si prodigue de soi-même, de nos jours". He lamented our pervasive indifference, but it was a spectacle which provided the necessary dimensions for the exercise of his genius,—Romantic impulses struggling upright against the horizontal levelling blast,while it snatches the words from their lips, obliterates the pretty effect of their most heart-felt gestures. So, half emergent into the contemporary light of day, half sunk in the shadows of a fabulous past, I detect a further resemblance between the creatures of Villiers' fancy and the innumerable populace of Constantin Guys, since they, too, like passers-by who step out of the darkness onto the gas-lit threshold of some café or restaurant, glancing about for a friend—they, too, present a facet of their persons harshly illuminated, keeping the rest submerged in the mysterious quality of their vocation or type, the *lorette* standing as at the mouthway of some interminable corridor, the "carriage-lady" amid vanished elegances in dim backward perspective.

Such protagonists demand an appropriate setting, neither vapourish nor excessively distinct, and this, with the good-grace born of his particular temperament, the passion for material splendour, "un mobilier riche", which appears to have haunted the creative genius of the nineteenth century, Villiers accorded them, joining yet one more cell to the ramifications of his original design,—the enormous chambers of some Armorican manor-house, so lofty that near the ceiling always floats a damp layer of mist, where in profound retirement dwells the dowager-duchess of Kerléanor: or another, probably not far removed along the coast, supreme retreat of Valleran de Villethéars and Paule de Luçanges, "deux beaux êtres humains", "deux âmes bien nées", who had met and joined hands under the mild beam of the evening-star of Melancholy: Torquemada's palace, the uneven marble slabs of the cold floor sibilant at the Grand Inquisitor's sandalled tread: or, in Paris, "un vaste hôtel seigneurial", lozenge-shaped hatchment dominating the cavernous porte-cochère, drawn curtains and silent rooms attesting its mistress' death, where the Comte d'Athol paces to and fro with rigid gravity, dismisses the servants, locks the doors, preparing finally to immerse his life in the memory of the defunct: an immemorial German castle, a supper of famous courtesans, Solomon's throne-room—scenes no matter what, nor thronged by what company as long as their endowment is immoderate, men and women whose emotional selves are so highly charged that they can be relied on to shed a pure, unqualified brilliance, creatures of heroic capacity but of reserve no less distinguished, reserve, for example, as consummate as that displayed during the story called *Sentimentalisme* in the person of its main actor, Maximilien de W. . . , his high, peaked shoulders and ghostly *haut de forme* silhouetted black against a nocturnal *féerie* of sliding lights and errant shadows:

Par un soir de printemps, deux jeunes gens bien élevés, Lucienne Émery et le comte Maximilien de W. . . , étaient assis sous les grands arbres d'une avenue des Champs-Élysées.

Lucienne est cette belle jeune femme à jamais parée de toilettes noires, dont le visage est d'une pâleur de marbre et dont l'histoire est inconnue.

Maximilien, dont nous avons appris la fin tragique, *était* un poète d'un talent merveilleux. De plus, il était bien fait, et de manières accomplies. Ses yeux reflétaient la lumière intellectuelle, charmants, mais, comme des pierreries, un peu froids.

Leur intimité datait de six mois à peine.

Ce soir-là, donc, ils regardaient, en silence, les vagues silhouettes des voitures, des ombres, des promeneurs.

The fall of those introductory lines is specially characteristic, as well as the general proposition they make. *"Deux jeunes gens bien élevés"* . . . the insistence, within so very short a space, on the couple's good-breeding, from another pen would be ridiculous. Here it is a further refinement of the author's style, a symptom of his constant desire to reduce human figures to their different essences; and, as far as good breeding does, or ideally *should*, effect a simplification by the removal of false shames, trivial ambitions and uneasy alertness, we may grant that it is aesthetically legitimate. But then, notice the careful antithesis of the verbs,—"est" and, italicised, *"était"*, since the

narrative reaches its climax in Maximilien's suicide,
—and the careful spacing of the nouns—"des voitures, des ombres, des promeneurs". Stretching out
and clasping her lover's hand, Lucienne begins to
"catechise him at length,—whether he does not think
that great artists, like Maximilien himself say, must
lose the faculty of feeling deeply: "Il semblerait,
alors, à voir la froide mesure de vos mouvements,
que vous ne palpitez que par courtoisie. L'Art, sans
doute, vous poursuit d'une préoccupation constante
jusque dans l'amour et dans la douleur. A force
d'analyser les complexités de ces mêmes sentiments,
vous craignez trop de ne pas être parfait dans vos
manifestations, n'est-ce pas? . . . de manquer d'exactitude dans l'exposé de votre trouble? . . ."—ingenious piece of feminine verbiage intended to steel the
hapless young man for a terrible avowal;—she has
pledged an assignation with his successor, a certain
M. de Rostanges, whom I conceive as the "superbe
viveur, fatal et discret", of one of Laforgue's unwritten stories, at half-past eleven this very evening.
Ostensibly unperturbed, the young man pursues his
defence. I transcribe its melodious conclusion:

Hélas! nous sommes pareils à ces cristaux puissants où
dort, en Orient, le pur esprit des roses mortes et qui sont
hermétiquement voilés d'une triple enveloppe de cire, d'or
et de parchemin.

Une seule larme de leur essence,—de cette essence con-
servée ainsi dans la grande amphore précieuse (fortune de

toute une race et que l'on se transmet, par héritage, comme un trésor sacré tout béni par les aïeux),—suffit à pénétrer bien des mesures d'eau claire, je vous assure, Lucienne! Et celles-ci, à leur tour, suffisent à embaumer bien des demeures, bien des tombeaux, durant de longues années! . . .

Dandysme—a word I have hitherto, and of intention, suppressed—will here, no doubt, leap uninvited into the mind of every reader whose ear is sensitive enough, after receiving the attack of that memorable cadence, to record the least impression of beauty. O the declining emphasis of "Bien des demeures, bien des tombeaux . . .", . . . "Je vous assure, Lucienne", . . . its timid, interpellatory note, as though he knew his trouble were all thrown away on a stupid woman and it were mainly the sacred obligation of eloquence which urged him to proceed! Marshalling alongside this passage a couple of previous citations,—"Je sens, alors, que je porte dans mon âme" . . . and "D'ailleurs que nous importe la justice", . . . their combined vigour, I like to think, clarifying perhaps the rather nebulous outlines of my thesis, will throw a flood of light across the perplexed geography of Villiers' genius, and reconcile the master of prose, conscientious and almost fanatical, with the *blagueur* and artificer of tragedies in a single line, his gift of magnificent assurance with the writer who presently sounded such profundities of disillusion that he no longer esteemed it worth his while to take up a pen and nightly squandered his imaginative substance in talk, among a hungry troop of journalists, scribbling down his stories under the conveniently overhanging ledge of the marble table-top, Villiers understanding their manœuvre and smiling,— a *dandy*, in fact, of neo-Romantic mould, who suffered to the full the swarm of painful anomalies his profession of faith, he realised, must necessarily evoke, who supported them with a grace more arrogant even than Maximilien himself knew how to employ . . .

To Maximilien I return. The fatal hour, half-past eleven, closes in. He rises, beckons a carriage, smiles, watches it disappear, makes his way homeward towards the Etoile, writes, cuts the pages of a new book, presently gets up. Having confronted us with the *décor* of inhuman fortitude, it remains for Villiers to show the human anguish of wings and dressing-rooms. Thereon depends the success or failure of his story. We expect no moving rodomontade, clenched fingers, lacerated palms, the Romantic excess of grief which reminds us of nothing so much as of disordered bed-linen, a soaked-pocket handkerchief, a towel drooping its fringes in a basin of cloudy water, a comb with clogged teeth, the morning dejection of the alcove;—but the chastity of Maximilien's despair must be eloquent of its force, his restraint of its finality:

Deux heures de la nuit sonnèrent: il s'étira.

Ce battement de cœur est, vraiment, insupportable! murmura-t-il.

"*Qualis artifex*. . . ." That background of nervous anguish or nervous exaltation, cunningly instilled, excuses or more than excuses the complete absence of anecdotal or "psychological" support. Villiers' prose method was poetic. It was a prose justification of the renowned Symbolist maxim that literature should find a second birth in her affinities with music. It was contained in a *dandysme* which refused the cumbrous, *voyant* habiliments of an inferior story-teller's apparel. Its approach pre-eminently was allusive, and, if it availed itself of the fruits of observation, it was only when they had been so worked over by intelligence that the grain of the raw material was quite obliterated. Villiers' power to supply the colour of an emotion, while sparing us the accidents of its temporal shape, proceeds not directly from analysis but depends on analysis for its remote foundation, just as some act of extreme physical dexterity may depend on a course of manual exercises once learned and immediately forgotten. Qualifying his point of departure, we might resort to an atavistic comparison,—a richly gifted prince of the Church he may have numbered in his heredity, a prelate of wide culture skilled in worldly manipulations of the human conscience, his dogmatic basis fallen away, leaving

123

behind it an unexhausted fund of surprise at the strangeness of the confessions it is his privilege to overhear. Surprise, seldom incredulity ... and when a successful young actress, this moment back from a hurried visit to her suburban cottage, was ushered into his presence, so palpably ruffled, her fur-trimmed velvets, pleated muff of pearl-grey silk, "gantée d'un très foncé violet", "au minois chiffonné, à la coiffure ébouriffée", he would be amused but hardly startled to learn how the delicious warmth she had experienced giving a ragged mendicant ten francs and his corresponding warmth at receiving it, the cumulative hypocrisy, in fact, of any philan-thropic gesture, *Les Délices d'une bonne œuvre*, had been gradually replaced by a sensation of over-whelming weakness, how it had conducted them by imperceptible degrees to a complete and passionate fusion of the kindliness they severally felt, benefac-tress and beneficiary subsiding with common ardour into a bed of sweet-smelling new-mown hay piled on the roadside.... And then, subsequently, record-ing the occurrence, a comprehension of human life, extensive yet sedulously limited, would enable him to reproduce the delicate transitions his narrative required; at every turn he would reveal a contradic-tion, a link between ostensibly conflicting moods, which is nevertheless consistent as soon as you come to ponder it, the sensual indulgence of charity so-called disinterested, a frigid propriety often inherent in vice.

So Villiers unfolded the story of *Les Demoiselles de Bienfilatre*. Conflicting worlds of "virtue" and "vice" must bring forth a conflicting array of standards, appropriate to the warring universes and exactly contradictory in every detail. Error! the naturalist objects, and the Goncourts, admirable representatives of naturalism of the secondary rank, make a convincing demonstration of supposed good and evil inextricably mingling motives. But Villiers persisted, and, to enjoy his story, you have to allow his premise; the respectability of a "disreputable woman" is the reverse, the concave side, so to speak, of a "respectable woman's" virtue. A respectable prostitute "falls" if she resign her body with any other view except the hope of gain, even under the license of a "poor but honest" marriage. That was the dilemma of the Demoiselles de Bienfilatre. The solution of their difficulties I shall be well advised to leave intact in its exquisite crystal phial.

So he lightened *Maryelle* of the secret of her recovered *pudeur*, as adroitly and unobtrusively as he removed her cloak. Her tale was not recommended by novelty. "C'est seulement *sa manière d'être banale* qui m'a semblé assez extraordinaire." Proportionately Villiers' manner of being commonplace astonishes us. We see the vulgar wallpaper of a private room, the curtains, lustre, glasses, the cigar ash falling, its heavy, inert flakes on the carpets and on the covers of the chairs. We see our imagined prelate, this time thoroughly disguised, no cardinal but "mauvais prêtre", *mondain* but in a fashion slightly superannuated, as though his valet had brought out of a lowest drawer and carefully brushed the garments he used to sport when he was an adolescent, when Romanticism was yet abroad,— still, carrying off his incognito with grace, "le loup de velours d'un impénétrable et gracieux pseudonymat", the narrator's troublesome half-anonymous *I*. Confronting him, we see his companion, a mercenary, lively, sentimental nature, leaning forward on her elbows, and lavish of her new-found happiness in the agreeably tuned jargon, the "gentil babil" her vis-à-vis' alchemy will presently change to gold. She is neither the Romantic hetaira nor quite the *cocotte*, *putain*, *lorette* of Second Empire and Third Republic. Not idealised or distorted from the semblance of human flesh and blood, she has been etherealised, reduced to an essential wraith.

And since the marvellous thus intimately encroaches upon the commonplace, it is with hesitation, a defensive wrinkle of doubt, that we exchange gas-light for torch-light, the urban pastoral of the crepuscular Bois, the vulgarly papered cell of a restaurant's private-room for the cyclopean masonry

THE DANCER: Drawing by Constantin Guys

of a mediaeval stronghold, lugubriously islanded among the "indeterminate tree-summits" of the Black Forest. But is not *Axël*, the critic wonders, Maximilien's blood-brother? He has the nobility, the reserve, the indomitable pride. Seclusion has given his habits a savage, feudal cast. He is a great hunter; his walls are nailed with trophies, an eagle with its vast spread of mouldering wings, aurochs' horns, the skins of bears. A profound student, too. "Toute verbe", Janus, his master of occult science, teaches him, "dans le cercle de son action crée ce qu'il exprime"—a literary faith which belongs as much to his begetter as to the young huntsman and occultist, a faith which gives this long poetic play a sublimity and uniformity it would otherwise not achieve, without which it might share the failure of *Le Nouveau Monde*, *La Révolte* and kindred products of Villiers' soaring dramatic ambition. If it is doubtfully, hesitantly a critic enters the humid shadows of Axël's castle and of Sara's convent, he stays a voluntary prisoner. Suspicious of the virginal huntsman with the eagle's feather in his cap, of the rebellious novice brandishing a jewelled poignard, by them he is possessed, accompanies their descent from *The Religious World* and *The World of Occult Knowledge* to their eventual meeting-place, *Le Monde Passionnel*, witnesses their discovery of the ancestral hoard, "ce torrentiel ruissellement de lueurs", hears the faint tintinnabulation of the scattered, dancing pearls, "tintant sur le marbre des tombes et rejaillissant, en gerbes d'éblouissantes étincelles . . . avec le crépitement d'un incendie", the thunderous escape of the heaped coin, "tonnantes et sonnantes cataractes d'or liquide", mindful perhaps of the "sterile riches of forgotten kings" which loaded Villiers' own breast and lighting on a hidden, ironic significance: Villiers' father also had been an impassioned "fouilleur de trésors": Villiers' penury was due to a life-long hopeless search for subterranean gold.

Beyond the region of heroic-ironic fancies lies the territory of Villiers' grotesque and comic invention. *L'Eve future* is a story of modern Galatea, but the fantasy is a little *voulue*, a little mechanical, and, as I have attempted to trace it, Galatea seems to stand a little outside the circuit of Villiers' mind. Her charm is present, but external, a figurine from the workshop of a Jules Verne turned poet. Incidental are the pleasures of the work, though occasionally rare, and I transcribe an arraignment of human stupidity by the inventor, Edison, "Phonograph's Papa", the legitimate complaint of an artist who does not resent criticism but deplores its puny reach, the timidity of its assault:

Ainsi, j'eusse blâmé, par exemple, le Phonographe, de son impuissance à reproduire, en tant que *bruits*, le bruit . . . de la Chute de l'Empire romain . . . les bruits qui courent . . .

les silences *éloquents* . . . et, en fait des *voix*, de qu'il ne peut clicher ni la voix de la conscience? . . . ni la voix—du sang? ni tous ces mots merveilleux qu'on *prête* aux grands hommes . . . ni le *Chante du Cygne* . . . ni les sous-*entendus?*

Altogether different is the case of M. le docteur *Tribulat Bonhomet*. For he is the necessary complement and appendage of Maximilien, of Axël, Ahriman to their Ormazd, a figure compact of darkness, self-sufficiency, as they are of light; what Blake called the "human Spectre"; a diabolic M. Prudhomme, M. Tout-le-Monde, democrat, agnostic, the treasure-house of his bosom fast sealed up and utterly vacant, but who knows the trick of ringing down his pewter coin with sententious emphasis; an authoritative manufacturer of phrases, citizen of Europe, "man of the world", professor of physiology, vaunted melomaniac whose pastime it is to murder swans ("ces chers virtuoses"), that he may enjoy their dying threnodies ("qu'il est doux d'encourager les artistes!"), patron of "good literature", enemy of poets, scientific observer, dilettante of human aberrations, his penetrative skill glancing back baffled only before the opaque, blue-lensed glasses of Madame veuve Claire Lenoir: Villiers coarsened, thickened, hugely magnified his monster, swathed his "osseous and gigantic" frame in a solid waterproof, shod him in iron-soled india-rubber boots, coiffed him in a vast brimmed tall-hat, equipped his murderous grasp with antiquarian steel gauntlets well-fitted for the elastic gullet of a fear-maddened swan,—by contrast subtilizing and attenuating the sympathetic phantom of Claire Lenoir,—till he had reared himself a Memnon of unbelief, a colossus exactly calculated to emit the right dissentient hum on the touch of any venturous dawning ray; maniac labour not unworthy to be compared with the prodigious toil which had lifted towards the firmament Bouvard and Pecuchet, —those cloud-capped pyramids!—this superb sentinel I erect to mark the bound and survey the inadequacies of my brief, presumptuous expedition,— against so many statues of agate a massive column of salt.

JULES LAFORGUE

WHILE Villiers, among how many others, is a writer you are better advised to study than to follow, because the age most likely to follow him, of all periods in our life, is least likely to grasp the essentials of his style, the work of Jules Laforgue remains sufficiently unscalable by imitators to make the fatigues of a close reading productive of some good. But then, by such various paths is a writer approached. There are paths which double upon themselves and loop backwards on the starting point. And there are paths which gradually deflect from their original centre and lead out again towards open country. The smallness of Laforgue's achievement, judging in areas of print, necessitates a more complicated ramification of alleyways and, since the objective is slighter, a more wary and more delicate advance by his critic. Perhaps an attempt at translation, begun hurriedly when much of his work was still unknown, can provide a suitable base, and this is my apology for the accompanying notes. Translation, like botanizing and plant-drawing, usually futile enough in the matter of results, will sometimes marvellously fertilize an acquaintance with the plant, the poem or the story it is required to transpose. Faults and subtleties, so intimately connected, appear where earlier glances, anxious to comprehend the whole, have accomplished a ruthless simplification. Division takes place and reunion as well. Details fuse together and reappear under the form of general peculiarities. Suspicions are dissipated or confirmed. The geography of *Moralités légendaires*, its special vocabulary, the astonishing legerdemain with which it is handled, the felicities and revealed imperfections of its method, may be used to qualify a cautious appreciation of the poems.

Now Laforgue derived largely, but most often from himself. A considerable distance was travelled during the eight or nine years of his poetical life, and the record of his journey is uninterrupted. He never allowed a procession, so to speak, of unwritten poems, to break the sequence of his written work. The sequence is clear, very clear. An excessively limited swarm of words, busy round an equally limited stock of images—that must be the complaint of his detractors, a half-truth which does not lack significance, even to those who most admire. Words, images and entire friezes of imagery recur, not once or twice. Thus to limit himself was, I believe, a voluntary condition of his success. But the last assertion needs support, and I hazard a reference back to the biographical materials at our command.

The life of Jules Laforgue—are we not favoured in that?—offers very little purchase to curiosity. We have evidence to dispel the mournful attraction of an artist's personal career. He was born abroad, in Montevideo, was brought up in the provinces of France, lived through several years of deep obscurity in Paris, was appointed reader in the Empress Augusta's household, and died, soon after his marriage, at the age of twenty-seven. We possess the bare outline of his movements and as many letters as go to fill a hundred pages of ordinary type. Yet the moral being who emerges is not at all vague; and the impressions M. Gustave Kahn lets escape him, narrating his first encounter with Laforgue in *Symbolistes et Décadents*, add definition to the already definite structure. M. Kahn emits a note of ingenuous surprise: Laforgue attended the meetings of a society he and Kahn frequented, less, it would seem, with the intention of drinking and making a noise than of hearing poetry read aloud. And generally, his aspect was "un peu clergyman et correct, un peu trop pour le milieu". As though the irritating restraint of Laforgue's presence urged him to stress the perceptible affectation which enshrined it, he finds room in his portrait to include the useless book Laforgue carried when they walked the streets—"Promenades, où un livre à la main, quelque mauvais Taine d'art ou quelque bouquin de philosophie, lui paraissait néces-

saire à son maintien" . . . Generally, an air of restraint, of conscious rectitude and decorum, a perceptible dandyism—the reverse side, the sensitive,
absurd cortex of that upright sensibility his letters
reveal, the letters to his sister and their continual
"soigne-toi, soigne-toi surtout" and "console-toi,
résigne-toi . . . je vais gagner largement ma vie,
je vais m'occuper de Charles et d'Adrien"—(his
brothers; M. Laforgue, "un excellent père . . . bien
qu'il ait trop lu Jean-Jacques Rousseau", had unexpectedly died)—"et avant longtemps nous vivrons
ensemble, et je te ferai une existence heureuse, si du
moins il en peut être une pour toi" . . . Or he wrote
of his own discomfiture with the kind of serious
irony presently familiarised by his work, how he is
too poor to dine in restaurants and how, evading the
satiric eye of the concierge, he bought his food and
carried it up to his room, hidden in his coat-pocket,
was at pains to get rid of a melon-rind, went out
again and, walking to and fro beneath the arcades of
the Odéon, managed to drop it on the ground. He
described his reception at the German court. "Letters
of an almost virginal naïveté", Mr. Arthur Symons
calls them, and yet, supposing his letters ought to be
characterized by any other epithet than *commonplace*
or *charming*, it is hardly their innocence you would
single out. Their innocence is at least as calculating
as the innocence, say for example, of a young girl.

And I should be rather inclined to comment on the economy of effort they display—no prodigality in rebellious sentiments, aspirations, regrets, no undergraduate expense in cumbrous, widely advertised trivialities, bought at a loss and carelessly entered to Experience.

Library toil and the habit of research postulate a good many sources; yet the influences he suffered were mainly local. He borrowed here and there, and remained a conscious debtor. An influence, brooding over the poetical life of the latter part of the nineteenth century, which has been extended into the twentieth, refining and continuing to strengthen its control, Laforgue could not, nor would have wished to avoid. His obvious debt to Baudelaire is demonstrated by the earliest poems of the collected edition, but you can recognize a profounder kinship where Laforgue had no opportunity of derivation or subsequent comparison, in Baudelaire's private journal, the eleventh paragraph of the *Fusées*, a passage which runs:

Ces beaux et grands navires, imperceptiblement balancés (dandinés) sur les eaux tranquilles, ces robustes navires, à l'air désœuvré et nostalgique, ne nous disent-ils pas dans une langue muette: Quand partons-nous pour le bonheur?

That is a re-evocation of manner and content. It illuminates the harbour scene of *Les Deux Pigeons*, echoing a recurrent theme in Baudelaire's verse, the theme of

Emporte-moi, wagon, enlève-moi, frégate,

and the splendid *Invitation au Voyage*.

Laforgue's wandering island must be anchored alongside the rooted promontory of Baudelaire. A modern critic has recently stretched an analogy between the experimentation of Laforgue and Corbière and the essays of the group of seventeenth century English writers loosely called Metaphysical Poets. The analogy might be furthered. Let Baudelaire represent Elizabethan eloquence and Laforgue a metaphysical poet, acknowledging its power but zealously concerned to refract and diversify its effects. True innovator, he comes not to destroy but to perpetuate an admired tradition, to perpetuate by apparent schism. Or he comes to destroy and build again, within as short a sum of days as his own weakness and the difficulties of the contract allow him. And now compare a technical device. Re-read the outstanding poems of Marvell and King, the complete text of Donne, trying to analyse their compulsive charm. That charm, I believe, consists not more often in the surprises of a new-refreshed diction than in the adaptability of its pace. Marvell's *Coy Mistress*, King's *Exequy*, can they not of themselves determine the musical accompaniment of an imaginary voice?

Lines differ one from another in the various temperatures of excitement each line expresses.

> . . . With all the speed
> Desire can make or sorrows breed . . .

and

> But heark! My pulse like a soft Drum
> *Beats* my approach, *tells* Thee I come

are two degrees of precipitancy, proceeding to a contrasted measure. The poet distinguishes between the quality and pressure of emotion. So Laforgue exercised his diction, till it could exactly cover the requirement of his theme. In *Derniers Vers* you apprehend the moment of coincidence. Or a very narrow margin of virtuosity overlaps and is waveringly apparent round the substantial nucleus of the poem. Laforgue's death put aside the threat unrealized; he might have taken pleasure in the triumphant solution of his aesthetic problem, not in the problem itself.

I am anticipating. Laforgue made his first recorded essays with solid, imitative grace. Now and again, he used a derived first line to launch individual divagations:

> Sous le ciel pluvieux noyé de brumes sales . . .

and

> Voici venir le Soir, doux au vieillard lubrique . . .

are Baudelairean formulae. The imitative catch of

the last is repeated, during the course of the sonnet, by an entire quatrain:

> C'est l'heure où l'enfant prie, où Paris-lupanar
> Jette sur le pavé de chaque boulevard
> Ses filles aux seins froids qui, sous le gaz blafard,
> Voguent, flairant de l'œil un mâle de hasard . . .

And later, desperately taking courage of his own immaturity, he wrote:

> Je puis mourir demain et je n'ai pas aimé.
> Mes lèvres n'ont jamais touché lèvres de femme,
> Nulle ne m'a donné dans un regard son âme,
> Nulle ne m'a tenu contre son cœur pâmé . . .

Plaint a discernment sharp as Laforgue's, if casually emboldened to utter, subsequently cancels with abrupt ridicule. The *form* of the complaint is cancelled. Nostalgia defies suppression. A permanent feature of his landscape?—Why then, the poet's sensibility is bound to assimilate it. Approaching an impersonal goal, Laforgue clothed his obsessions in a mythological propriety:

> Il était un roi de Thulé,
>   Immaculé,
> Qui loin des jupes et des choses,
> Pleurait sur la métempsychose
>   Des lys en roses,
>   Et quel palais!

Rarification of the form stabilized and lent the transitory emotion an enduring value. Self-limitation entailed this reward. A Romantic exploits the status of being a poet: "There is a position ready fortified, which shall guarantee my sensitiveness. I shall suffer, I shall suffer never doubt, yet the mode of suffering is consecrated. My shrill reprisals will but swell an interminable series" . . . Poets who have abandoned adolescent sensitiveness for mature sensibility (sensibility is capable of growth; sensitiveness is a preliminary excavation, that you can continue—to the bone) prefer to renounce the shadowy privileges of their state, a necessary piece of arrogance, piece of effrontery which may lead after them the benefits they have rejected, as some prophet-king despises the enjoyment of kingdom, sets his trust in the company of fortunate spirits, to bring water from the rock, furnish him music and join their wings in a shelter above his head. Thus Laforgue renounced the attitude or, call it what you like, the altitude of a professing versifier.

A poet is no less dishonest who denies and would obliterate the character of his obsessions, than absurd if he credits them with a superlative importance. Laforgue bettered the customary process of development, did not presumptuously throw away one illusion against a second (an illusory disillusionment) but treasured both, since relatively both are of equal significance and value. His allusive wealth increased and free-swimming illusions,—like the *Medusae* of the aquarium tank, through whose translucent bodies you can watch the rhythm of digestion and elimination,—shone through by intelligence, showed a greater clarity and an undiminished delicacy of outline. For "knowledge", we remember, can make a sapient use of "ignorance": witness the Metaphysical poet's

> At the *round* earth's imagin'd corners, blow
> Your trumpets, Angells . . .

—And so Laforgue's verse was gradually charged, as it were, by transfigured films of commonplace, by illusions of his own adolescence, by illusions of foreign growth and by the cadence and refrains of popular songs. A crystalline, impersonal beauty he sought to give his adolescent phantasms and prepossessions. Thence rose his lunar mythology.

> Women, that (of all things made of nothing)
> Are the most perfect idols of the moon,
> (Or still-unweaned sweet mooncalves with white faces)
> Not only are patterns of change to men,
> But as the tender moonshine of their beauties
> Clears or is cloudy, make men glad or sad . . .

But, whereas the imagery of adolescence reflects only a desire to escape, to forget its proper limitations, "*n'importe où, hors du monde*", Laforgue's imagery was circumscribed and fixed by self-ridicule as by the dark circle of his optic glass:

Quand ce jeune homm' rentra chez lui,
Quand ce jeune homm' rentra chez lui;
Il prit à deux son vieux crâne,
Qui de science était un puits!
Crâne,
Riche crâne,
Entends-tu la Folie qui plane?
Et qui demande le cordon,
Digue-dondaine, digue-dondaine,
Et qui demande le cordon . . .

Poor young man, whose head is a reservoir of science that he finds himself incompetent to turn to any immediate use, whose genial preoccupations are with his own life and the instinct that urges him to propagate it, with the disparity between his circumstance and his hypothetical abilities, between his atrocious idealism and the opposite sex towards which it is helplessly directed! "Et les hommes de génie!" Lohengrin demands, "Pourquoi les faites-vous souffrir tout particulièrement, les hommes de génie? D'où, cet instinct qui confond le penseur à certaines heures?" . . . "Je ne sais pas, puisque c'est un instinct", Elsa riposts, sullenly crouched in the bed beside him.

And:—

Dans les jardins
De nos instincts,
Allons cueiller
De quoi guérir

Hamlet murmurs, during one of those unpremeditated lapses into verse which enliven the text of *Moralités légendaires*. But the bunch of healing simples of Laforgue's male protagonist gathers, always shelters the "insane root". Romantic passion may be discredited; it is still far from anachronism. A conflict admitting no solution, an imprisoned whirlwind of irresistible desire and inevitable disappointment, swells the lyric frame of every story. Lohengrin rescues Elsa, when the ecclesiastic cruelty of her neighbours prepares to blind her. Lohengrin is an idealist. He is the "Lily of future crusades for the emancipation of Woman"—(Laforgue's *Sur la Femme* embodies the same contradiction)—but he sweats at the sound of the marriage anthem and, kneeling before the altar, moistens the altar-cloth with "long, lustral tears". O the indecent facility of their honeymoon in the officially subsidized Nuptial Villa, picturesque thatch, vulgar weathercock, names and dates scratched with a diamond on the mirrors! "Cela sent la fosse commune", Lohengrin declares, attempting a gallant compromise:

> Nul Absolu;
> Des compromis;
> Tout est pas plus;
> Tout est permis.

Yet Elsa, "nubile à croquer", what has she to offer him except the horrifying concavity of a complete devotion? Even her nursery-rhyme lullabies hide an

epithalamic tang. "Seriez-vous libidineuse, Elsa?"—
"J'ignore le sens de ce mot—Ah! mais, chantez
donc, vous, alors!" With an exemplary elocution,
Lohengrin recalls the King of Thule. Eventually,
like *Pierrot Fumiste*, he fails in his duty as a *husband*
and a *man*. The swan-chariot answers his distress,
bursts open the casement among a cyclone of lunar
magic and ravishes him away "towards the Heights
of Metaphysical Love, towards those glacier-mirrors
that never a young girl can breathe upon and cloud,
tracing with a finger in the steam her name and the
date".

Salome and Saint John, Andromeda and her
Monster, Pan and Syrinx prompted variations. The
Moon presides. She is the patroness of women, spins
the monthly wheel to which they are bound, sym-
bolises inconstancy, dispenses transcendental attractions from a barren shell. It would be hard to leave
the poet without a homage to his *décor*. As if *décor*
and theme were separable! . . . as if you could separate the poet and the prose-writer! Prose encour-
aged Laforgue where verse intimidates. And prose
fostered an occasional redundancy which the discipline of verse would have spared. Verse sharpened
his ear, and there is an endless amusement in the
extravagant conjunction of syllables:

. . . à l'horizon, les flots jusque-là enchantés d'accalmies,
exécutant vers elle (vers la Lune, of course) un va-et-vient

berceur, ostensiblement berceur, comme la suppliant de se laisser un peu choir, ce soir, pour voir, qu'on la dorloterait si nuitament! . . .

Hitherto the story has gone forward in a substantial prose, pointed and immensely clarified by arduous verse training. Elsa's trial—we have reverted to *Lohengrin, Fils de Parsifal*—takes place under an overweening harvest-moon, "la belle pleine-lune vieil-or, ahurie, hallucinante, palpable, ronde", from which Laforgue distilled the splendour of that hour when Night and Day mingle with a disconcerting crepuscular radiance:

Irrecoverable, so much as in imagination, are the evenings of the Grand Sacrifice! . . .

Naturally, the rise of the First Full Moon, implacable divinity, had been chosen for the degradation of the Vestal Elsa, in the cathedral square of Our Lady, while every bell was tolling out *Nox Irae*, in full sight of the eternal ocean of fine evenings.

Facing one another, on opposite dais, inviolably draped in linen, were set the White Council and the Corporation of Vestals; between these institutions, a whispering throng of people, the whole attendance ranged in semi-circle, all afoot, and their eyes, blue, green and grey, strained expectantly in full sight of the superhuman ocean of fine evenings.

It is still broad day; not one indulgent breeze came to torment the short flames of the candles.

For whom is it they wait?

Heavens, how white and wild all looks just now, upon the verge of this solemn ocean basin! How far from home I seem! . . .

There appears over the enchanted horizon Our Lady.

None other than the fair, old-golden full moon, alarmed, delusive, palpable and round! So close, you would say it was a work of Man, some experiment in aerostatics of latter days (yes, a globe so artless in its enormity as to be like an untethered balloon).

As always, it strikes cold . . .

*　　　*　　　*

Sur la Femme is a commentary on Laforgue's personages and their theme, *Paysages et Impressions* on the mica-brilliance of their environment. Ideas or physical sensations, his sensibility was impartial in its appetite. Torments, caused by an idea, send off more effulgent sparkles of wit and observation, that is all. Like Callot—I claim the indulgence comparisons of art require—like the French draughtsman, he relished the potential comedies of suffering. And, as Callot, in a plate which happens to be near my hand and depicts the torture of offenders in a public square, townspeople, peasants riding asses, gentlemen on horseback severally agog to watch a heretic burned, a man broken, torn asunder, decapitated, birched, flogged, hoisted on the *estrapade*, has sympathetically lavished his fantastic skill among the melodramatic cloaks of the riders, the lean rumps of the horses and the writhings of the criminal, Laforgue concerned himself with other arenas of suffering—with a transfigured Baden-Baden and the anguish of "nervous cases", who make a queer noise of automatic swallowing as they hastily leave the concert hall, who twist suddenly about as though their nape had been grazed by an invisible assailant, and, in the secret recesses of the woods, sow the immemorial ravines with fragments of torn-up letters.

For the prose-writer's expressed intentions, I quote from *Pensées et Paradoxes*:

"Écrire une prose très claire, très simple (mais gardant toutes ses richesses), contournée non péniblement mais naïvement, du français d'Africaine géniale, du français de Christ. *Et y ajouter par des images hors de notre répertoire français, tout en restant directement humaines.*" The sentence italicized seems a very just estimate of his actual achievement. Delicacy, too, neatness, freshness, fineness—commendatory substantives the want of a more exact critical vocabulary may permit to stand—he desired and got:

"Dans le roman" (he wrote in *Paysages et Impressions*), "O linge fin! nul ne t'a chanté. Vivre n'importe comment, être tragique ou sceptique, aller ici et là, voyager, s'éterniser dans des trous, faire des scènes ou en supporter, etc. . . . et l'on sort un mouchoir de batiste, souple et calin aux doigts, et le soir on rumine sa journée sur l'oreiller de fine toile vergée, dans les draps fins—mousseline rude—comme du papier et qui ne servent pas assez pour perdre leur plis en carrés de l'armoire—et la cou-

verture capitonnée à multitude de fleurettes jon-
quille . . ."

With each new effort, the poet tended to epitom-
ize what had gone before. *Le Concile féerique* con-
densed earlier material. *Derniers Vers*, a sequence of
twelve poems, conveniently read as one poem in
twelve parts, closed the procession. The form had
been revolutionized. But so powerless is the form,
the exterior form, "free" or "traditional", in the last
resort either to excuse or condemn, that the attentive
ear will hardly mark an alteration, and, if you listen
for a peculiar cadence, your ear recovers it wearing
an unaccustomed suppleness and ease, and barely
emphasizes the formal revolution on which it depends. Too often Laforgue's poems suggest the in-
definite postponement of an attempt. It is as though
the writer were content with fluency. *Derniers Vers*
reach after classicism—classicism understood not
only as the classical sententiousness of expression,
chiefest virtue of eighteenth-century verse, but as the
completeness of expression attained by a masterly
innovator of any school, who strikes away from
tradition, whose curve of development, insensibly
pressing round again into contact, exchanges a long
electric flash with the past.

Baudelaire is related to the drama of the seventeenth century, perhaps more intimately than Remy
de Gourmont believed; Laforgue is related to Baude-

laire. Illustrative of his nearly achieved classicism, I should quote such a line as:

Simple et sans foi comme un bonjour

and, because it reflects on a paragraph of Baudelaire's journal I have previously transcribed, these lines from the tenth poem:

J'aurai passé ma vie le long des quais
A faillir m'embarquer
Dans de bien funestes histoires,
Tout cela pour l'amour
De mon cœur fou de la gloire d'amour.

Oh! qu'ils sont pittoresques les trains manqués! . . .

Oh! qu'ils sont "A bientôt! à bientôt!"
Les bateaux
Du bout de la jetée . . .!
De la jetée charpentée
Contre la mer,
Comme ma chair
Contre l'amour.

The purpose of a brief survey must be to hint at certain resemblances and affinities in the author's work, and give a tentative description of its *climate*. We need not attribute doctrine, except where it is explicitly asserted. Laforgue's nature was to avoid pronouncements, at most to parody them. When the hereditary rulers of the White Esoteric Islands, Laforgue's speculative retreat, received the crimson-cheeked Satraps of the North, representatives of prevailing culture, and when they had made their guests visit the Aquarium, recollected by Laforgue from an aquarium at Berlin, the dignitary called Pope des Neiges delivered a cautionary harangue:

"Ni jour, ni nuit, Messieurs, ni hiver, ni printemps, ni été, ni automne, et autres girouettes. Aimer, rêver, sans changer de place, au frais des imperturbables cécités. O monde de satisfaits, vous êtes dans la béatitude aveugle et silencieuse, et nous, nous desséchons de fringales supra-terrestres.... Mais, ô villégiatures sous-marines, nous savons pour nos fringales supraterrestres deux régals de votre trempe: la face de la trop aimée qui sur l'oreiller s'est close, bandeaux plats agglutinés des sueurs dernières, bouche blessée montrant sa pâle denture dans un rayon d'aquarium de la Lune (oh, ne cueillez, ne cueillez!)—et la Lune même, ce tournesol jaune, aplati, desséché à force d'agnosticisme (Oh! tâchez, tâchez de cueillir!)."

Ce fut donc l'Aquarium; *mais est-ce que ces princes étrangers comprirent?*

*   *   *

So this was the Aquarium, Laforgue concluded, but how much of it did the stranger princes understand? How much have his readers understood? How much, I wonder, did his contemporaries? Like all retiring and self-denigratory spirits, Laforgue runs a constant risk of being accepted at his own very modest valuation;—an obscure young man pitifully aspiring towards excellence, an adolescent relegated to inertia and the doubtful pains and satisfactions of his adolescent day-dreams not only, he realises, by the outward unkindness of his fortune, but, more definitely, by some principle of weakness existing in himself:

> Or, pas le cœur de me marier,
> Étant, moi, au fond, trop méprisable!

Yet the consciousness of insignificance did not enrage him as, for example, it had enraged and exasperated poor Tristan Corbière. Corbière, too, had his self-pitying, self-condemnatory refrain; "Je suis si laid", he would sigh. Laforgue was the first to differentiate between their respective manners of complaint. "Corbière papillote", he wrote, answering some newspaper critic, "et je ronronne." Corbière flutters; his sense of insufficiency inspires him to a perpetual, wearying movement. Comparatively, I am placid; I purr: "Je vis d'une philosophie absolue et non des tics; je suis bon à tous . . ." Quiet application, a long process of self-discipline had made it possible for him to stand apart and appreciate the harrowing spectacle of ambitious and defeated youth, both in the capacities of actor and of reflective, impersonal spectator. He mingled the bitterness of defeat and the pleasure which comes from another sort of victory; he was detached. . . . And thus it is that, besides mirroring the futile discomfitures of adolescence, Laforgue's imagination, like one of those small circular glasses which epitomise and enrich the scattered features of some sprawling and chaotic room, supplies also a dignified context, a sober and consistent ground. Trifle as he please then, yet Laforgue is seldom trivial. He is the supreme sentimentalist, but he is never lacrymose. An immense underlying seriousness guarantees the ebullitions of his effervescent, abounding humour. Even his sensual reveries seem to have been laid up like pressed blossoms, dried and preserved between the chapters of an innate puritanism.

CORBIÈRE : RIMBAUD : MALLARMÉ

Iᴛ is a feature of the modern universe that, in en-
larging its territories, it has also impaired our sense
of distance; it has immensely extended the range of
our perplexities and, with the same gradual movement, has weakened our appreciation of their seriousness. Like children who prefer to the elaborate
gifts showered upon them by their elders such simple
yet ingenious playthings as they can improvise themselves, an artist would gladly renounce the expensive
over-elaborate paraphernalia of modern civilisation
and modern barbary in exchange for the plainer,
purer, cruder symbolism of the ancient world. From
the ponderous ramification of a modern army, the
bustle of its multiple units, the clatter and swarm of
worsted-grey troops piled among their baggages
along the cold concrete expanse of a railway platform, the poet derives an impression of less stirring
energy, of a lesser magnitude and strength of purpose than from the contemplation of one of those
old battle-pieces where the opponents are represented as diced irregularly across the field, woolly
clouds of smoke alternating with tight-set thickets
and wide-flung crescents of lowered steel,—from a
squadron of horsemen or the clump of tapering

spears which forbid the passage of an "alien river".
... Literature, which offers us—we may believe it
or not, as we please—the spectacle of a continued,
always partially frustrated effort towards certain formal standards of perfection, will also provide us with
a running criticism upon the life of its own times.
Every period furnishes its own type, in whose person
is summed up and epitomized the larger triumphs
and larger maladies of his epoch. These heroic figures
resemble the water-mark which underlies a printed
page; an examination of them, held up to the light,
will enhance the value and significance of the printed
design. The historical water-mark is, indeed, an in-
tegral if not a controlling factor in the literary composition by which it is so nearly obliterated. Turn
the next page,—it has altered; it changes, grows, till
finally it has accomplished a complete transmogrifi-
cation of its original traits. Both images deserve careful scrutiny; and since, of the three writers with
whom I hope to deal, two at least have received a
somewhat intensive *literary* examination at the hands
of previous critics, it may be excusable to vary the
form of the examination, and enquire whether we
cannot extract their "fabulous" or "heroic" as well
as their literary and merely aesthetic content. They
are writers, portions, that is to say, of a literature
which we can acknowledge or reject at our own good
pleasure; they are also legendary figures whom, willy-

nilly, consciously or unconsciously, we *must* accept; they are a fraction of ourselves, of our attitudes, our ambitions, our affections and antipathies,—figures that, because we can command no choice in matters of our inheritance, we had, in fact, unwittingly accepted some long while before we were ever called upon to register our final decision.

*   *   *

When Verlaine first celebrated his achievement in *Les Poètes maudits*, Tristan Corbière was already almost forgotten. He had died in 1875 and, though two years earlier a publisher had issued his volume of collected poems, that publisher's subsequent bankruptcy and the dispersal of his stock had wrought *Les Amours jaunes* down into an obscurity from which it seemed probable that their author would never rise again. He might, at best, have hoped that his pages would be idly turned over in their quayside retirement by some curious amateur of the period; they would have added another volume to the surprising and discouraging mass of miscellaneous literature, precious and ephemeral *bouquins*, reviews and manifestoes of every colour, yellow, red and blue, as short-lived as summer moths, in which the intense spiritual activity of the decade had found its ultimate expression. His book would, no doubt, have been included by M. Gustave Kahn in that dusty moth-case he calls *Symbolistes et Décadents*,—which, of itself, is a sufficiently final interment. But Pol Kalig, like Corbière a Breton, and his cousin and friend, had handed *Les Amours jaunes* to Léo Trézenik, the director of *Lutèce*; Trézenik had showed it to Verlaine, and Verlaine, setting to work the very same evening on which it was brought to his notice, had composed his passionate eulogy: "Tristan Corbière fut un Breton, un marin et le dédaigneux par excellence, *aes triplex*. . . ." Himself *par excellence* the type of immensely sympathetic, immensely intuitive, strictly unintelligent writer, the poet for whom the exercise of his genius resembles the instinctive exercise of an animal function, *le pauvre Lélian* was particularly apt to recognise and, recognising, to salute a poet whose verses were no less harsh and unequivocally designed than his own were melodious and *nuancé*. As a rhymer and prosodist, Verlaine observed, Corbière was far from impeccable. It was his superlative vigour, the maritime *brusquerie* of his attack which conquered the critic's admiration. Thus, while the general direction of his criticism is sound, the terms under which it is set forth are exceedingly diffuse and wordy; rather than give a clear definition of the qualities he admired, Verlaine was inclined to envelop his subject in a cloud of rhetorically conceived adulation. "A desperate lover of the sea", he wrote, "one that only mounted its back during the stormiest weather, a spirited cavalier on this the most spirited of saddle-horses". . . . Here the personal legend seems to obsess him, and he is concerned further to spin out and interweave that network of personal mythology in which, as in a glutinous web, each of us hopes to catch the wandering interest of our contemporaries and ensnare the imagined suffrage of the future. Well, Corbière, too, had his vanity, but lacked the requisite degree of self-deception which makes vanity formidable. He was a *poseur*, it is true; he was also a literary *sans-culotte* of the race that, while it possesses the badges of respectability, prefers not to wear them; it flaunts its affectations abroad, elevated like a banner. Over the heads of the gaping, trousered multitude, it lets them stream empty and ridiculous in the blast.

The conduct of his life had not lacked an element of perversity; he had enjoyed a moderate degree of personal freedom, but, refusing to confine his explorations within the easy circular range on which he could pasture undisturbed, he had deliberately sought out the limitations of his tether-rope, the point at which it began to grow taut, the point at which it absolutely forbade any forward progress, and had determined that the fraction of an inch gained upon the axis would be worth the whole un-impeded segment from which he had averted his eyes. Then, if the chain still held,—what he had lost upon the radius of the circle he would make up in the excessive velocity with which he rounded its circumference. His exuberance betrays itself as somewhat strained and artificial; his affectation often reveals the constant tension which it was meant to hide. But the capricious *verve*, the impetuosity which so delight our friends are generally the despair of our real intimates. "His baptismal name", Corbière's mother has written, "was Edouard, but he must needs choose a second and more eccentric, like himself. . . . This son might have been our glory, had they not provoked, flattered and spoiled him in the world of artists in Paris. . . . He was only thirty when he died". . . . "Je suis à Dubois dont on fait les cercueils!" he had informed her comfortably from his nursing-home.

Their sentimental fragrance apart, how eloquent both messages are,—Madame Corbière's ineffective, disappointed tenderness and the admirable yet unkind irony with which her son announces his own approaching decease,—of an entire chapter of modern literary development! For the history of nineteenth-century literature, English and French alike, is, in some large measure, the history of a young man not without fortune and opportunities, but whose means are neither so elastic that he can afford to give his inclinations full scope, and thus aspire to reach eventual calm by way of complete satiety, nor yet so curtailed that the question of possible escape never presents itself to his mind at all. The origins of literature are the ritual operations of the magician; the key-stone of the magician's power is a promise that what circumstance denies the natural, supernatural knowledge may still effect. Thus literature's highest, as well as its most debased, forms are a channel in which irrealizable desires seek an illusory fulfilment. Few hands have not, at one time or another, played and fumbled with the key, but, as adolescence passes, the shadow of the prison-vault, far from thickening and becoming more oppressive, seems actually to lighten and disclose new prospects of solider, less vaporous satisfactions. Beside the single thrush, tightly grasped and, indeed, hardly struggling in the fingers, it is an uncommon appetite which will reach after two nightingales declaiming in a spiny thicket, or two swans in euphonious death-throes among the tangled white and purple flag-sheaves of the river bank. We must assume the intervention of an alien yet decisive factor; Plutus is not a divinity who has the official right of entrance to the Muses' mountain-side confabulation. Present he is, though;—and pervasive, here as elsewhere, rivals the omnipresence of Universal Pan. His influence, no doubt, might be exaggerated as hitherto it has been entirely ignored. And yet, admittedly, there is some very real and permanent connection subsisting between the aesthetic, moral and the economic or financial history of a given period. The historian of Romanticism, at least,—the future historian, like a careful gardener who, while he unearths a plant from its bed, disinters with equal scrupulousness its uttermost, nearly invisible fibres and the sturdy tap-roots on which the main current of its life depends,—must take into account not only the rapid and brilliant process of emancipation which that movement implies, but also a slower, much more inglorious process of political and financial emancipation of which the movement he depicts was an incident, though (he may object) the sole incident worth recording. For the purposes of such a work, the theme of the accompanying essays would provide the matter of a foot-note or of a brief appendix; because our ways do, in some sort, bear a parallel direction, I may be allowed parenthetically to anticipate a line of approach along which, as I conceive it, such a historian might think good to make his first piratical inroads into the territories of nineteenth-century literature.

Power, he would begin, whether it is political, social or financial, is, so to speak, its own poetry, its own music and its own drama. Of inestimable service as they have always been to art, a twentieth-century capitalist or eighteenth-century nobleman or princeling, when personally he adventures into the foreign plane of art, must set out in the same spirit in which he adds another half-acre to dominions already almost as large as a county or feudal estates already exceeding the breadth of several minor kingdoms. He draws down over his head the firmament of music or poetry, but must surely be conscious all the while of merely adding to the wide, plentifully wooded and watered expanse of soil, from which his pleasures, his consequence and even his name itself is derived, another and superfluous kingdom, hypothetical, phantasmagoric, its value unknown, its boundaries notoriously unstable. Upon the microcosm of lands and houses, his possessions, which imitate a smaller pattern of the universe, why superimpose the trifling microcosm of the mind? Is not literature, he might ponder, primarily the consolation of the dispossessed, secondarily the entertainment of Dives? But then, after all, it is none of Lazarus' business either! Before extreme indigence the slope rises up so sharp and painful; and, if apparently but a short way ahead, the frontier-mark dividing *him that hath and to whom it shall be given* from *him that hath not and from whom it shall be taken away even that which he hath* suggests the prospects of an arduous and nearly impossible climb. It is just about this frontier, on the contrary, a little above it sometimes or a little below, now among the *petits bourgeois*, now among the *hobereaux*, the squireens and the squirelings, Byron and Shelley, Messieurs de Vigny and de Lamartine, that literature is usually recruited. The feudal oak-tree is seldom visited by its afflatus;—or it elects the waifs of the oak-grove, its wastrels and its strays, the un-hampered and independent, the responsive because unattached,—Alfred de Musset, a graceful winged seed, equipped for immediate flight![1]

And it is precisely the doubtful nature of their position—affluence lying just above them, out of reach; indigence, thank heaven, just below—that has made the *bourgeoisie*, by temperament so much less given to extravagances of conduct than their distant "superiors" and "inferiors", the never-failing source of political and aesthetic upheavals. "Il faut perdre un préjugé baudelair-ien",—M. Jean Cocteau writes in *Le Coq et l'Arlequin*; "Baudelaire est un bourgeois. La bourgeoisie est la grande souche de France; tous nos artistes en sortent. . . . Il y a une maison, une lampe, une soupe . . . derrière toute œuvre impor-tante de chez nous",—a lamp and a soup-tureen, whether it is the lamp, comforter and tutelary divin-ity of a crowded household, under whose hateful glow the young *bourgeois* sits down to read and

[1] . . . lui, qui n'avait eu ni logis ni maîtresse,
Qui vivait en plein air, en défiant son sort,
Et qui laissait le vent secouer sa jeunesse,
Comme une feuille sèche au pied d'un arbre mort!

draw, or the soup-tureen whose aroma, seeking out
and hanging in the furthest corners of their cramped
Parisian flat, belies the pretensions of some impover-
ished family of country noblemen, drifted to the
town,—a family which Maupassant represented often
and with loving minuteness: the ineffectual father,
the mother much suffering and faded, the unmar-
riageable, pathetic daughters, their impatient, proud,
ambitious and shamefaced son! For, though apparently inert, self-contented, slow moving, year by
year the huge middle-class throws off into the void
its emancipated, educated, yet unsatisfied and deeply
resentful progeny. They have had the leisure to de-
velop tastes which circumstance forbids they should
enjoy; they have arrived at a sense of their human
and eternal importance that nothing in the economic
comedy of which they are the wire-pulled automata
can enable them to maintain. Their latent, inherited
idealism will debar them from snatching at the prospect of a successful career; and, while the growth of
some great national legend, the Napoleonic legend
for example, may provide a temporary outlet and
foster in its shadow a short-lived crop of Romantic
opportunists of the sort typified by Stendhal in the
hero of *Le Rouge et le Noir*, the evident failure of
their contest against circumstance, and the eventual
disappearance of the legend which shelters them,
will presently thrust the generation back again into

the unique sphere of activity, elastic and vague enough to include its heterogeneous requirements.

So it is on to the plane of literature there bounds that dangerous and incalculable being, the emancipated *fils de famille*! Here decaying titles get themselves fresh emblazoned and regilded,—much to the derision and disgust of the urban aristocracy, who, like Madame de Villeparisis in *A l'Ombre des jeunes filles en fleurs*, have ransacked a profounder vein of *snobisme*. Here, too, in the fructifying atmosphere of the capital, old, ignoble surnames fall away; the husk, *Gérard Labrunie*, withers and curls back, making room for the triumphant and melodious *Gérard de Nerval*; simple *Isidore Ducasse* is reborn under the magniloquent title of *le comte de Lautréamont*. There is no end to such transformations; every man comes to literature in search of his missing attributes. Hephaistos, clumsy artisan god, is in quest of the suppleness of gait and erectness of carriage with which his mother did not endow him; his wife, "l'éternelle Vénus, caprice, hystérie . . .", blunders across the horizon, picking up with her, as she flies, the predestined rags-and-tatters of the modern female novelist. . . . But, because the origins of literature are haphazard, because its growth has, in the extreme, proved casual and desultory, this acknowledged fact will by no means help an opponent to a specious dismissal of its products, nor yet will it warrant his relegating literature to the category of human affairs which have a relative, a merely documentary significance. We should envisage its processes, upon the other hand, as being rather more gradual, rather less voluntary than, perhaps, during the first delighted acquaintance with the work of genius, we may have rashly supposed. The creator himself seems less individual; he is an assemblage, the rallying-point of innumerable sympathies and aspirations (the general property of his age) which the peculiar magnetism of his temperament collects and centralizes in the compass of a single brain; he is a township, centralizing and epitomizing the arts and prosperity of its surrounding districts; his individual intelligence is the vaguely understood common-will of an entire polypus mass; his individual products, as distinct as a coral branch, finely curved, rosy and cold, are, after all, the sum-total of their confused deposits.

And hence it comes about, that the verses of Corbière, and of the other poets associated with the word *Symbolist*, are expressive of a movement involving the fate of whole generations. The storm-wind of Romanticism, while it still blew strong, had supplied in genial violence, in impetus, what it had neglected to give in any concrete aim. Its devotees received a free passage through life, charioted upon the skirts of the tornado, and, if they pleased to take it, the necessary ritual formula of a dignified and tragic release. Romanticism, Remy de Gourmont has pointed out in an amusing essay, exercised a nation-wide as well as a purely local effect. It supported the giant enthusiasms and, sometimes, the giant *niaiseries* of such men as Hugo and Théophile Gautier; but it was also the stimulus—to untold raptures and untold despair—of a thousand thousand attorney's clerks and high-minded apothecary's assistants whom their fate had cast away into mean lodgings in the blind, shuttered streets of obscure French provincial towns. Suicide followed in its track; the Russian student of yesterday, the modern American undergraduate infected with Behaviourist leanings (Mr. Wyndham Lewis informs us), are impelled towards suicide by a conviction that "life is dark and worthless", by an apprehension of its triviality; these unnamed and unremembered self-slayers discharged their pistols or kicked away their stools in an apprehension of its fullness and of the tragic intensity of their lot. The passions they aroused had at last over-whelmed them; or suicide was a deliberately con-temptuous gesture and they relieved the human stage of a weight heavier, they felt, than its wretched worm-eaten boards could carry for very long. Cer-tainly, from whatever motive, their exit had nothing akin to the final dispositions of the modern suicide, apathetically inhaling coal-gas or deliberately miscalculating his sleeping-draught. . . . For Romanticism lends a sense of personal consequence, a sense of unflagging speed preserved in perpetuity by a very real disinclination ever to reach any one definite goal. They had discovered, or thought they had discovered, these lesser intelligences, the secret of perpetual emotion. Their cult had deteriorated into the art of exciting the highest and most pleasurable degree of emotional stress at the least possible expense of intellectual fatigue. The heart is a well, bottomless. . . . Let it be an artesian well, then, always brimming over, its waters always cool and bubbling toward our lips,—raised from the depths without troublesome preliminary strainings against the winch-head of thought!

But that a time would ever come when "the thoughts of a dry brain in a dry season" had replaced the vernal "impulses of the heart", and the Mental Traveller looking around him could distinguish—

> . . . no water but only rock
> Rock and no water and the sandy road
> The road winding above among the mountains

to a Romantic soothsayer might have appeared almost inconceivable. Yet, while Emma Bovary was tending her cactus-plants, corresponding with her young lover across the village street and burning Algerian pastilles, though sensibilities as backward, as vulgarly greedy of sensation as hers, could still experience its devastating impact, the vigour of the movement had declined and it was fast dying away. Imaginary characters, it may be argued, are untrustworthy witnesses in a question of historical event, since they are at once more and less solid than the historical personages amid whom they are set down; they cannot be dated—they are timeless. If that be so, let the critic accept Emma's name as personifying the class of readers who, when the remote outflung ripple of some great literary movement has at length reached and subjected them, can be relied upon to give a sure sign that, at its centre and origin, the agitation has already subsided;—it has, in fact, become vulgarized beyond repair. Its mighty protagonists had outlived the movement they began. 1848, climax of Romantic-Revolutionary enthusiasm, had failed in all its main objects. Former insurgents looked back on their activities with a sort of ironic tolerance; the very excess of their ridiculousness, Baudelaire wrote, had made those few days charming and memorable. They had invoked the people, only to take up arms against them, shoot, imprison and ship them in chains overseas; they had dethroned Louis-Philippe, only to clear his road for a future Emperor of the French.

Action was discredited, nor could their literary admirers pretend that, of the two most prominent poet-statesmen who had taken a share in the handling of the recent crisis, either Lamartine or Victor Hugo had left upon the history of France or in the minds of their contemporaries an impression which was likely to be very permanent. Lamartine shrank into himself, disappointed; Hugo retired into voluntary exile. . . . Thus, by the recital of facts and through the symbolism of proper names, we attempt to endow with substance and exactitude a very gradual alteration of the literary climate. Under another figure, let us say that when the fevers of Romanticism had died down, they were succeeded in the corporate body by a lowering of temperature far beneath the normal, which brought with it, as such sudden falls of temperature often do, a condition of immensely heightened sensitiveness, but also a considerable decrease of the sufferer's enthusiasm and vitality:

> Quand Rolla sur les toits vit le soleil paraître,
> Il alla s'appuyer au bord de la fenêtre . . .

The chilly gust of morning air that greeted him, Musset should have concluded if he was to have given his poetic melodrama a prophetic cast, numbing his cheeks and finger-nails, deprived him at a single breath of the long-cherished ambition to take his own life. Hollowing his shoulders, folding across his bosom the thin lapels of his evening coat, he left the room and wandered forth on to the unswept pavement of the streets. He had cast out the sphinx of self-destruction, and its vacant niche was presently filled again by a monster less hasty-tempered, less bloodthirsty, but, proportionately, more vigilant, clearer-eyed. This spirit of intensive self-mistrust and self-ridicule, implacable foe to all pretensions of personal Romanticism, indefatigable examiner of all those various proposals of Romantic action which a lively and impetuous nature may suggest, delighting to reveal them as the threadbare *pretexts* that they are,—though it must be credited with having inspired the extreme, timorous fragility which is the chief characteristic of many of Laforgue's and Corbière's poems, should also receive the credit of having dictated the peculiar scrupulous sincerity which usually distinguishes the form. And so, disdaining any pretence:

> Mon père (un dur par timidité)
> Est mort avec un profil sévère;
> J'avais presque pas connu ma mère,
> Et donc vers vingt ans je suis resté

—Laforgue wrote: you know the worst now, hypocritical reader, you who affect to consider the poet a being of different, more godlike stuff than yourself!

> . . . je vivotte, vivotte,
> Bon girouette aux trent'-six saisons.

Thence the position of a modern writer, M. André Gide, who announces with naïve impudicity, that he intends to speak at length of the delicate repercussions upon his brain of an exacting physical constitution: "Je vais parler longuement de mon corps . . ."—is but a short march distant. Literature, like an invading host that the first *élan* of victory carries over an area wider than it can practicably defend, and which is thereafter obliged to fall back and consolidate its forces by deliberately narrowing the scope of its aggression, felt, still feels perhaps, the need of contracting its bulk, of rigorously curtailing the exuberant outline of its frontier. And so, to the stinging military music of its preferred measures, Corbière's verse, as well as proclaiming several brief adventurous forays into previously unexplored territory, also announces an orderly and even vindictive withdrawal from a sector of spurious enthusiasms latterly much fought across and heaped with the Romantic dead:

> Qu'ils se payent des républiques,
> Hommes libres!—carcan au cou—
> Qu'ils peuplent leurs nids domestiques! . . .
> — Moi je suis le maigre coucou.

>   *   *   *

> — Ma Patrie . . . elle est par le monde;
> Et, puisque la planète est ronde,
> Je ne crains pas d'en voir le bout . . .
> Ma patrie est où je la plante:
> Terre ou mer, elle est sous la plante
> De mes pieds—quand je suis debout.

Conscious at the time of fighting a rearguard action, stubbornly withdrawing under a banner which bears the spectacular inscription: *Je m'en fous*, Corbière, and other poets like him, could not so easily wean away their sympathies from the vaster mass of human beings whose preoccupations, in the political and moral sphere, Romanticism, for all its much-advertised opposition to the *bourgeoisie* and to *bourgeois* standards, had championed and made its own. Was it not something, that a poet should have enjoyed the requisite degree of self-deception, the requisite headiness, headlong unthinking courage, which propels a man up the steps into the rostrum, or emboldens him to step down and canvass unashamedly among the crowd? Was that not something they might regret? For, rooted deeply in every artist's nature, beside an instinctive leaning towards the few who share his interests, is an impulse towards the many who do not, coupled very often with a suppressed abhorrence of the intellectual oligarchy to which he belongs. The most unpoetical living creature, Keats has said in one of his letters, is the poet; and many other writers have experienced a similar aversion from their kind. Appreciative of sound, resilient flesh and of high-coloured exuberantly coursing blood, a poet is naturally intolerant of these mere husks of men, each carrying about with him, like a burdensome parasite, a memory of

the work upon which he is actually engaged, as well
as the additional dragging weight of future projects
and dangling past disappointments. Their conversation is tedious; their professions of friendship, he
knows, are dangerous and undependable. Every
promise given has been given subject only to ratifica-
tion by their parasitic master; every association
formed has been formed only for so long as he nods
his approval;—a state of affairs which, when once it
has been grasped, will, no doubt, explain the somewhat indecent precipitancy that many artists display
as soon as wealth or elegance has beckoned them. It
may also help us to understand the fascination exercised over minds, otherwise delicate and finely
balanced, by a life of extreme squalor, *la nostalgie de
la boue*, the charm of brutal and outlandish contacts
in the propinquity of danger and suffering. For, like
Edward FitzGerald (though whether or not sharing
FitzGerald's emotional bias seems obscure), Corbière
had spent several years cradled passionately among
the wallowing aquatic monsters of the northern seas.
He had been "the winds' tennis ball", had courted
dangerous currents and reefs; he had visited the
sailors' brothels and drinking-places, and had written
the collections of verse called *Armor* and *Gens de mer*.
Superbly vigorous essays! And yet, underlying his
celebration of *Le bossu Bitor*,—Bitor the hunchback,
throwing away his stockingful of savings in the

"bagne-lupanar" Breton sailors named *Cap-Horn*,—
of *Le Douanier*, a salt-dried and sun-bitten angel—

> Qui flânes dans la tempête,
> Sans auréole à la tête,
> Sans aile à ton habit bleu! . . .

—there is an ironic second-thought which sets
off these solid, insentient companions against the
writer's own sensitive instability. Roscoff and the
sea—his spirited and splendid courser,—and *Le
Négrier*—his boat in which he tempted its gigantic
reprisals,—his seafaring acquaintance, excellent play-
fellows and play-ground, no doubt! Yet he is obliged
to leave them all behind, to admit that his chief concern is with his own existence, and to set his face
towards the capital,—towards those natural enemies
his fellow *littérateurs*,—where his destiny as a poet
will be realized. Then, if his life in Brittany had been
erratic, denizen of a ruined tower, and only less
rigorously disapproved by his few neighbours than,
even at that time, Corbière was by himself, when
finally he had reached Paris, and gained a *milieu*
which condoned and sometimes positively encour-
aged his idiosyncrasies, he could not rest till he had,
as far as possible, stepped clear of and provocatively
spurned aside the last conventional restraint. A man
needs shelter; yes, one bare monastic cell. He needs
a bed; but the bed, with its full complement of
blankets, sheets, pillow-cases, had gained the sinister

reputation of being a main stronghold of the domestic virtues. Families are founded there! It is a kind of symbolic nest—

Qu'ils peuplent leurs nids domestiques! . . .

The meagre cuckoo, with whose fate Corbière had identified his own, as often as he does not accept the hospitality of another bird's coverlet, is content to spend his restless nights stretched out upon a hard, wooden-topped coffer. Money, too, he needs. But, for the *fils de famille*, however decisively he has broken apart from the parental stock, a pittance is seldom lacking. The thin golden stream nourishes and warms him. Carried in his pockets though, money is cumbersome and might confer a sense of obligation. Such occasional *louis* as reached Corbière's hand, he left scattered with contemptuous liberality along the dusty shelf of his mantelpiece.

Thus lightly equipped, Corbière is a *franc-tireur* of the general literary retreat, a quickly moving rifleman, part soldier and part bandit or guerilla, who, beyond the rearguard even, relies for his continued safety upon the sureness of his aim and upon the unobtrusive swiftness with which his isolation enables him to move. Yet fluency, we know, is a dangerous gift; and, as opposed to this description, it will be only fair to adduce Corbière's colloquial mastery of language, which might perhaps be likened to the boldness of manner, the daring and ingenious choice of epithets, which so often redeem the work, their feeblest and least sustained efforts, of Elizabethan dramatic writers of the second rank. Without sacrificing the rhetorical homogeneity of a passage, Tourneur or Ford gives the separate lines which compose it each an individual poetic value—

> ... The poor benefit of a bewildering minute

—and yet the surpassing vividness of Tourneur's phrase does not detract from the forcefulness of the celebrated tirade in which it is included.

> Moi, mannequin muet, à fil banal!

—Corbière wrote, describing the torments suffered by a deaf man, isolated (he, too!) amid the absorbing pains and pleasures of the everyday world:

> Bonnet de laine grise enfoncé sur mon âme ...

But lest the reader should incontinently dismiss him as being one of those poets in whose work all the virtues are present except the saving principle which alone can give a composition unity, I must transcribe the exordium of his magnificent *Rapsodie du Sourd*:

> L'homme de l'art lui dit:—Fort bien, restons-en là.
> Le traitement est fait: vous êtes sourd. Voilà
> Comme quoi vous avez l'organe bien perdu.—
> Et lui comprit trop bien, n'ayant pas entendu.

"Eh bien, merci, Monsieur, vous qui daignez me rendre
La tête comme un bon cercueil.
Désormais, à crédit, je pourrai tout entendre
Avec un légitime orgueil. . . ."

"Rien d'impeccable . . . comme rimeur et comme prosodiste", as Verlaine admitted, Corbière's chief asset is the quality which Laforgue called his *chic*,— his mobility, that is to say, the elegant precision with which he brings down his quarry, the efficient grace with which he slopes his barrel and blows it into pieces like the pipe in a provincial shooting-gallery. "My beloved," exclaimed the unsuccessful marksman of Baudelaire's *Petits Poëmes en prose*, who had paused at a country shooting-booth to try his skill, his mistress by his side, "I shall now pretend that it is you!" Closing his eyes, he pierced the centre of the target. "I shall pretend, on the contrary, that it is myself!" Corbière would have answered; for unlike the clumsy, slow-fingered self-maceration of his Romantic predecessors, Corbière's self-destructive markmanship is extraordinarily brisk and adept. He does not hesitate or fumble:

Manque de savoir-vivre extrême—il survivait—
Et—manque de savoir-mourir—il écrivait

—sharp, tinkling repercussion! Or, bringing his weapon to the shoulder again, the poet tries a fusillade; twice Corbière wrote his epitaph,—*Épitaphe pour Tristan Joachim-Edouard Corbière, Philosophe,* and then, in smaller-lettered parenthesis, his description, *Epave*, *Mort-Né*:

> Mélange adultère de tout:
> De la fortune et pas le sou,
> De l'énergie et pas de force,
> La liberté, mais une entorse.
> Du cœur, du cœur! de l'âme, non—
> Des amis, pas un compagnon,
> De l'idée et pas une idée,
> De l'amour et pas une aimée,
> La paresse et pas le repos.
> Vertus chez lui furent défaut,
> Ame blasée inassouvie.
> Mort, mais pas guéri de la vie,
> Gâcheur de vie hors de propos,
> Le corps à sec et la tête ivre,
> Espérant, niant l'avenir,
> Il mourut en s'attendant vivre
> Et vécut s'attendant mourir.

There exists a second and more elaborate version,—more abundantly witty, perhaps, but, at the same time less easily defensible from those numerous reproaches to which the display of mere "wit" in a poet will always expose his verse.

> —Son seul regret fut de n'être pas sa maîtresse . . .

is a line, for example, predominantly *witty*; whereas, the peculiar virtue of Corbière's method does not so much lend his satire a poetic colouring, as emphatically forbid of any distinction between the two elements. A single explosion unites them; outrageous content delivered point-blank with startling lyrical aplomb:

> — Allons! la vie est une fille
> Qui m'a pris à son bon plaisir . . .
> Le mien, c'est: la mettre en guenille,
> La prostituer sans désir.

It is in the nature of the incalculable poetic spirit, that such violent assaults upon our complacency should, so to speak, penetrate without wounding; a far purer and profounder hush succeeds them than the factitious calm which they have interrupted.

*   *   *

The neighbourhood of a volcano is inspiriting. From a fragile platform of smoke, moored above its apex and imperceptibly swinging and veering upon the currents of the wind like a raft moored upon a stream, a sense of expectancy dominates and fertilises the surrounding landscape. This monstrous companion has worked its way so thoroughly into the minds of the inhabitants, that a critic would be hard put to it to understand their history and peculiar culture, unless it was by always keeping in imagination those gradually climbing slopes which tower without steepness over their heads, the mountain's enormous outflung shadow, the rosy intermittences of its midnight flash. . . . Ourselves the inheritors of a political tradition which could be expressed most appropriately in the least eventful of rolling curves, we shall do well to remember the rugged and volcanic profile of French political development;—for the Restoration of the Bourbons had been followed by the Hundred Days; some fifteen years later Charles X. had fallen and Louis-Philippe had taken his place; in 1848 the Monarchy had been succeeded by a Republic; after barely four years' life the Republic had succumbed to an Emperor;—with the accompaniment of unceasing invective, perpetual agitation against the existing order of things. And now, when an entire French army had surrendered and a Prussian army had reached the outskirts of the capital, the Empire, too, had fallen; Paris was in the hands of the Communards, and Arthur Rimbaud, a boy of sixteen, footsore and quite exhausted, approaching the first revolutionary patrol that he met, told them that he had walked sixty leagues,—the long road from Charleville, a little dead town near the Belgian frontier, to join them in their heroic defence. Once before he had left Charleville and gained Paris;—then he had been imprisoned and returned. Barely a fortnight passed—Rimbaud had enlisted in the ranks of the incendiaries, he used to inform his friends, participating in the destruction of several notable monuments—and he was again retracing his steps towards Charleville, ragged, destitute and solitary. His mother received him; the melancholy of a small provincial town swallowed him up. Childhood spent in the streets and squares of a small, undistinguished country-town! The loneliness such a childhood implies! And yet, perhaps, it is a more fruitful sort of loneliness than the loneliness which a young man afterwards learns to appreciate, mute and sullen, amid the intellectual society on which hitherto his adolescent day-dreams have been centred. Rimbaud's third visit to Paris, undertaken at the invitation of Paul Verlaine, who had read *Les Effarés* and *Les Premières Communions*, was the bitterest fiasco of all. Shy, insolent, *farouche*, Rimbaud lay sprawling among his benefactor's friends, blunted their gaiety with the display of heavy, brooding seriousness which was his natural element, pulled awry their gravity with a savage outburst of that sudden satirical humour in which, though normally sternfaced and preoccupied, he sometimes indulged his spleen. "Pisseurs de copie", he muttered, "salueurs des morts"—you journalists, busy at your daily excretion of the printed word; enlightened and emancipated spirits who canvass the respect of your fellows, lifting your hat-brims high as some unknown coffin trundles past! "Pustular toad!" his new acquaintance retaliated, resenting this truculent young *parvenu*, recognizing and resenting in him, no doubt, the angelic messenger of change. While, for his part, even the *bourgeois* of Charleville suited him better, Rimbaud must have reflected. It is our own, the *milieu* in which we have been brought up, however ostentatiously we thrust it behind us; the isolation of Madame Rimbaud's farm was preferable to the crowded antagonism he had found in Paris, his mother's taciturn ill-humour to the volubly annunciated dislike of Verlaine's friends; as opposed to the negative sympathy which unites us to our parents, the liveliest show of intellectual independence is often specious and ineffective.

So it is towards Charleville we must look. There Madame Rimbaud, excusably irritated but, at bottom, utterly unmoved by the vagaries of her younger son, went sternly and purposefully about her usual avocations. She was of peasant stock, *dévote*, a shrewd business-woman, a keen bargainer, an implacable parent, a hard and unforgiving wife. Her husband had been a spendthrift and a wanderer, the kind of man who cannot brook the ordinary domestic restraints. In her daughter, Isabelle, but softened and humanized, we divine the original harsh moral physiognomy of the older woman.[1] Isabelle, too, was a believer,—and with the added gift of tenderness; still, her faith was militant. It was like a weapon; she seems to have wrestled physically against her brother's blasphemous unbelief; his death-bed was

---

[1] Isabelle Rimbaud, *Reliques*, pp. 95-97.

the scene of her triumph. . . . "God be a thousand
times praised," she exclaims in a letter to her mother,
written on the twenty-eighth of October, 1891, "last
Sunday the greatest pleasure was mine which I shall
ever know. . . . No longer is it a poor erring and
suffering wretch who will pass away under my eyes:
it is a just man, a saint and a martyr, one of the elect.
. . . Merci, mon Dieu, merci!" But, in the same letter,
she is answering some enquiries Madame Rimbaud
had ventured with regard to the probable extent of
Arthur's fortune; while, elsewhere, she prefaces an
account of her brother's agony by a page or more of
solicitous questioning;—how does the harvest do,
the cows,—the little cow who is to calve in November? Let Madame Rimbaud sell her at the first
opportunity! Such a fusion of spiritual and practical
interests, far from weakening its effect, tends rather,
on the other hand, to strengthen and amplify the
significance of her faith. Implicit in her piety was the
invaluable power of concentration, so apt at driving
and, if necessary, goading, which achieves a moral
whole by sheer disregard of any formal distinction;
she deserts her *prie-dieu* for her work-table and her
ledger. The masterful ease with which she accom-
plishes this difficult transition is the solid basis upon
which her puritanism rests. Arthur, too, shared her
faculty of concentration. He shared, I believe, her
innate puritanism, though his puritanism had adopted

a form which was calculated to outrage the opinion of his contemporaries. He ran through the vicissitudes of unbelief with the rigid, unashamed and unequivocal dignity of an "upright soul" approaching its God.

Fables envelop him, Rimbaud has become the Chatterton of our days,—a figure that the youth-worshipper, the agnostic "professor of energy", the Jesuit schoolman, have each in turn loaded with the spurious attributes of their cult. After the most cursory examination of these fictions, with what a serious and compact grace the true Rimbaud, the Rimbaud of the poems and letters, stands up! No superfluity here, not even the velleities of youthful sentiment and appetite. A vague rumour of dissipations surrounds his life. He had a mistress in Charleville, Delahaye informs us, a girl of his own age; she had followed him to Paris and vanished suddenly into the throng; Rimbaud's face clouded when he mentioned her name. . . . Otherwise, his knowledge of the opposite sex would appear to have been limited by an absolute sentimental indifference,—by indifference or hatred:

> O mes petites amoureuses,
> Que je vous hais!

—the close atmosphere and squalid apparatus of a young girl's mind inspiring in Rimbaud a repug-

nance as vivid and as lasting as the delighted and in-
satiable curiosity which it provoked in Jules Laforgue.
He mistrusted those brief, dazzling contacts and,
when the first flush of sexual inquisitiveness had died
away, he ceased to desire them. His dissipations took
on an experimental cast; he submitted himself to the
contact of the outside world, ecstatic but impersonal,
like some heroic virgin who submits with fortitude to
her husband's soiling embrace. An inward reservation
guaranteed his integrity. Squeamish, amorous of a
thousand refinements which he had never enjoyed,—
wide, airy rooms, linen which does not exacerbate
but is so fine and soft that it mollifies and comforts
the skin,—the positive, deeply puritanical and ascetic
spirit which inhabited him would give him no peace,
till, again and again, he had tested his power of
resistance, tested and tried it to breaking-point. He
endured the promiscuity of barracks; he slept in
fields and under bridges; "hair and armpits full of
lice", he has described his condition. And yet, in
spite of frequent and deliberate attempts to brutalise
his native sensibility, . . . "se coucher dans la merde",
his moral equilibrium reasserted itself, the poetic
demon reaffirmed its sway,[1] and, choosing as his
subject the very humiliation he had undergone, the

[1] Verlaine, quoted by Delahaye: "L'extraordinaire macération
morale qu'il voulut subir l'affranchit de toute faiblesse, le libère de
toute manie. On ne trouverait pas dans son cœur une grossièreté ni
une tare."

degradation which had encrusted him so thickly but could by no means quite obscure his original candour, he wrote, for example, *Les Chercheuses de poux*,—a poem in which we read how, like the trodden blade of grass, painfully and gradually ticking back into the spiry elegance that its laws of growth ordain, beneath the women's silvery fingernails, their quick-drawn breath, the faint fluttering movement of their eyelashes, a profound calm once more takes possession of his spirit, a sweet quiescence delicious enough almost to bring tears:

> L'enfant se sent, selon la lenteur des caresses,
> Sourdre et mourir sans cesse un désir de pleurer.

A poet, already nearing the end of his maturity, already having conquered an astonishing richness and complexity of style, where he might expect a self-portrait which was wrinkled and faded and showed the trace of half a lifetime's unmitigated effort, sees the child that he still is, his own image, the reddened forehead,—"le front de l'enfant, plein de rouges tourmentes",—the hair damp and matted with dew. He is beyond himself, sees clearly and dispassionately, feels the childish relief from pain, the intensity of relief which only children enjoy. Genius, Baudelaire had said in a sentence I have quoted above, was "childhood recovered at will", the child's primitive impressionability exploited by adult nerves and intelligence. Then if, in flesh and blood, Rimbaud was the living realization of Baudelaire's critical sally, to Rimbaud, as he announced in one of his rare letters, dated from Charleville on the fifteenth of May, 1871, just before leaving his mother's house with the purpose of enlisting among the Communards, Baudelaire was the "king of poets" and first of *voyants* or visionary writers. He represented the seriousness, the concentration of design which Musset and Victor Hugo—"colossal vulgarian!"—so markedly lacked. Yet he condemns his aestheticism, thinks the beauty of his style overpraised. The poet must transform himself into a visionary; that, it is true, Baudelaire had done. He must attempt a systematic "*derangement* of all the senses"; he must seek to inoculate himself with every passion, every disease, emerging as the universal Sick Man, universal Criminal, universal Damned Soul, the supreme Scholar. Here we are reminded of a passage in which Baudelaire compares the poet to a Perpetual Convalescent, his preternaturally heightened sensitiveness maintained by a perpetual rhythm of illness and recovery. We remember Baudelaire's systematic abuse of drugs and the magnificent use he made of his resultant sensations. Well, Rimbaud must do likewise,—unspeakable torment which demands all his faith. That his poetic system required faith was, of course, a proof of its validity,—as befitted the descendant of pious women to whom any line of action that was naturally abhorrent would come naturally recommended.

He had inherited their piety,—to use "piety" in the older meaning of the word, their moral staunchness, their appreciation of any regimen which involved harsh and ungrateful effort. But he had also inherited their practical bent; he, too, reckoned, computed, counted up. Madame Rimbaud, while her son lay agonizing on his death-bed, had enquired from Isabelle what fortune she supposed Arthur would leave behind; some months earlier, while his bearers were hurrying him down towards the sea across the Abyssinian mountains, though he suffered atrocious pain, Rimbaud himself was industriously enquiring into the price of artificial limbs. And now, when he had reached Marseilles, his leg gone, his arm paralysed, the poet, turned colonial and man-of-affairs, who, I have suggested, had once surrendered the primitive, unwritten integrity of his spirit to the coarse embraces of life with the same cold, inflexible ardour as some devout, convent-bred girl might surrender her body, showed as jealous and tenacious a love of life as ever matron of the husband she has grown to value. "J'irai sous la terre", he cried frantically, "et toi, tu marcheras dans le soleil!" He raved, wept, blasphemed, vented his jealous fury and, struggling upright against his pillows, tried in vain to pick up the threads of business where he had dropped them a year ago; on the eve of his death, he was dictating an incoherent letter to a phantom correspondent, claiming an imaginary debt. The dying paralytic had still much in common with the young man who, between the ages of fifteen and twenty-three, had proved so avaricious of aesthetic and spiritual advancement. Already, on the occasion of the letter which gives a rough and tentative outline of his poetic system,—"the new literature" as he envisaged it,—a question arises whether literature, and literature alone, could afford his ambitions a permanent resting-place. Are its limitations not galling him already?—a reader asks. Does the spectre of Action not already haunt him? Suppose that the history of Rimbaud's verse may be arbitrarily divided into two periods;—then the culmination of the earlier period is in *Bateau ivre*, the poem written by a boy for whom the sea was unknown, a mere literary symbol, yet which "contained all the sea", Verlaine said,—its imagery dancing and boiling past our eyes like a kind of phosphorescent scum:

> Et, dès lors, je me suis baigné dans le poème
> De la mer infusé d'astres et lactescent. . . .

—the fluidity of the measure presently gathering volume and plunging over into the wildest and most fantastically conceived shapes:

Glaciers, soleils d'argent, flots nacreux, cieux de braises,
Échouages hideux au fond des golfes bruns
Où les serpents géants dévorés des punaises
Choient des arbres tordus avec de noirs parfums!

J'aurais voulu montrer aux enfants ces dorades
Du flot bleu, ces poissons d'or, ces poissons chantants.
Des écumes de fleurs ont béni mes dérades,
Et d'ineffables vents m'ont ailé par instants. . . .

—these ebullitions subsiding in a glaucous melancholy calm:

Si je désire une eau d'Europe, c'est la flache
Noire et froide où vers le crépuscule embaumé
Un enfant accroupi, plein de tristesse, lâche
Un bateau frêle comme un papillon de mai. . . .

—concluding with the superb invocation:

Est-ce en ces nuits sans fond que tu dors et t'exiles,
Million d'oiseaux d'or, ô future Vigueur?

—an invocation addressed to the future principle of Vigour, towards whose secret imminence his life would henceforth be oriented.

Bateau ivre he carried with him to Paris; there he met and captivated Verlaine, met and severally disgusted or annoyed the Parnassiens. His second period had begun. In Paris, he set to work again, but a difference was apparent, a difference already felt at Charleville, both as regards the manner and the purpose of what he wrote. Hitherto, the narrow limitations of his art had contented him. Literary ambition and the wider, world-aspiring ambition which included it, had, so to speak, coincided. Now a slight fissure appeared. For evidence of the impatient and suspicious attitude that Rimbaud assumed when considering the greater part of contemporary literature, the larger number of *littérateurs*,—Musset and Victor Hugo anathema! Gautier, Leconte de Lisle, Banville sufferable but no more—we need not go very far afield; his poems provide the internal evidence of a similar conflict. Then, whereas it is the peculiar virtue of great poetry that the forces it unchains should expend themselves within the compass of the given poem, like strong winds should blow themselves out, should leave no residuum but only a smooth-swept and vacant space where they have been, after their clangour a deep, pervasive hush, Rimbaud's earlier poems, even the finest among them, enclose elemental spirits of such undisciplined potency that the after-effect they make upon a reader's mind is often as chaotic as the beach after a storm, sharp under-foot with torn weed and broken shells. Like Marlowe, another poet whose verse, bloodshot with dreams of power, is the imperishable monument of a self-destructive, self-condemnatory spirit, Rimbaud took a definite pleasure in martyrizing his fluency against those fiery but, perhaps, slowly receding boundary-walls, *flammantia moenia,* which separate things possible from things impossible to express by words:

> If all the heavenly quintessence they still
> From their immortal flowers of poesy,
> Wherein, as in a mirror, we perceive
> The highest reaches of a human wit;
> If these had made one poem's period,
> And all combin'd in beauty's worthiness,
> Yet should there hover in their restless heads
> One thought, one grace, one wonder, at the least,
> Which into words no virtue can digest.

He knew the extent of his achievement; he was perfectly well aware, so he told his friend Delahaye, that *Bateau ivre* was a poem which, if it had equals and superiors, had certainly no equivalent; he knew that well! Praise would have been superfluous. Novel ambitions had taken hold of him. He still hoped to wring language for the very quintessence of expression; he wished himself a sort of actual physical control, a territorial dominion over the words he used. He had written the sonnet, *Voyelles*, allotted the separate vowels,—with the subconscious collaboration, it has latterly been pointed out, of an old spelling-book whose pictures had delighted his childhood,—their several colours and images; he had exhausted the treasures of classical literature and hoped to find the ultimate and mysterious formula, the secret of the final, irrefutable *Alchimie du Verbe*, transcribed more clearly and more simply in "old-fashioned books, Church Latin, ungrammatical pornographic works, superannuated novels, fairy-stories, children's tales, ancient operas, stupid catches, silly rhymes". He had anticipated the modern taste for "idiotic paintings, fan-lights, stage scenery, circus back-cloths, signboards, popular prints". His appetite for curious works of information the public librarian at Charleville,—or, multiplied in monstrous plural, librarians, *Les Assis*, who rise grumbling, gasping and belching when you ask them for a book,—had found it hard to assuage. Still his hunger and thirst persisted. Born during the Middle Ages, occultism, no doubt, would have been his refuge. Those labyrinthine underground chambers and corridors had connected art to art, science to science; they honeycombed the entire structure of human knowledge; they comprehended the highest and the lowest satisfactions; like a remote, always alluring, always retreating disc of light, they promised that the seeker after truth should one day step clear into the blinding noontide of omniscience. . . . If my reading of the poems is correct, at about the same time as he wrote *Bateau ivre*, just before leaving Charleville on his third visit to Paris, a conviction must have dawned across Rimbaud's mind,—a very gradual dawn, may be, a dawn which filters and irradiates the darkness but does not bring morning in a single stride,—that literature could never wholly

satisfy him. He did not discontinue his literary prac-
tices, but rather immersed himself in them the more
thoroughly. He worked hard; he tortured syllables,
decorating his conversation with words brutally and
deliberately twisted out of shape,—"*absomphe*, sauge
de glaciers", for absinthe, "*Pamerde*" for Paris. Yet
our genius will often make decisions of which we are
not immediately apprised; a load had been lifted
from his verse. The heavy accumulation of dreams
and temporal longings was drawn aside to wait another employment. His poems became slighter in
texture, but, proportionately, finer and more compact. A compressed and rarefied manner sometimes
makes them cryptic. Thus, in the beautiful lyric,
Bonheur, the exact incidence of "*le coq gaulois*" may
puzzle his reader's interpretative imagination. Re-
stored to its context in *Une Saison en Enfer*, the
reference is sufficiently plain. Rimbaud furnishes a
gloss, while in a passage taken from one of his letters
the gloss itself is further extended. "Nowadays", he
tells us, "I work at night, from midnight till five
o'clock in the morning." And he goes on to describe
how last month he had occupied an attic window,
overlooking the majestic foliage of huge trees; how,
at three o'clock, the candle had flickered and paled,[1]

[1] A quatre heures du matin, l'été,
Le sommeil d'amour dure encore.
Sous les bocages s'évapore
L'odeur du soir fêté.

the birds had all begun to sing at once, and he had put his work aside and sat, spitting down on to the tiles, looking across the trees into the narrow, deep city gardens, glancing up towards the transparent morning sky and watching the *lycée* opposite, absorbed in the odd, heavy-lidded slumber of a shuttered French house. Presently he would hear a noise of wheels along the boulevard,—"bruit saccadé, sonore, délicieux",—and, when the streets were already thinly peopled with workmen, would leave his room, buy a loaf of bread and drink greedily in the wine-shops; then back to his room and to sleep. But meantime, at his window, confronting the absolute repose of virgin dawn, he had recaptured the exquisite *solitariness* which is exhaled from some of the earliest verses he ever wrote:

> Par les soirs bleus d'été j'irai dans les sentiers,
> Picoté par les blés, fouler l'herbe menue:
> Rêveur, j'en sentirai la fraîcheur à mes pieds,
> Je laisserai le vent baigner ma tête nue!

Solitude within a solitude; silence only interrupted by the chill impersonal noise of birds, as though the multiplicity of warring noises had been reduced to these few thin trills and quavers; his interior quietude

---

> Là-bas, dans leur vaste chantier,
> Au soleil des Hespérides,
> Déjà s'agitent—en bras de chemise—
> Les Charpentiers . . .

similarly profound, the questions which engaged him equally simplified, he mused under the peaceful obsession of a single, all-sufficient problem: "Le Bonheur! Sa dent, douce à la mort, m'avertissait au chant du coq,—*ad matutinum*, au *Christus venit*,— dans les plus sombres villes:

> O saisons, ô châteaux!
> Quelle âme est sans défauts!
>
> J'ai fait la magique étude
> Du bonheur qu'aucun n'élude.
>
> Salut à lui chaque fois
> Que chante le coq gaulois. . . .

But dawn was succeeded by the heat and clamour of the day. His health was menaced, he believed. Like Gérard, he feared that his visions might overwhelm him;—"les hallucinations tourbillonnaient trop"; that, like Gérard, they might precipitate him finally into "the living sea of waking dreams", where reason and life itself would founder. Words were poisoning him; this commerce with words was as subtly degrading as the commerce of the flesh;—"O pureté! pureté!" Verlaine, unhappy and restive, had begged Rimbaud to leave Paris in his company; they would travel together, cross the sea perhaps, visit new cities. Rimbaud accepted; Paris and the midnight efforts which his existence there implied were fast becoming intolerable. He longed to know the sea, he remarked, as if it could have washed away a stain.

They over-ran the north; eventually they reached London, settling in a tall, sad-faced, evil-looking London house near the Tottenham Court Road. Their companionship had at first been care-free and light-hearted; but Verlaine, who, with his enormous convex forehead, his small, deeply sunk, crafty eyes and short, broad nose-ridge, so much resembled some venerable brute-god, a mask of Cheiron the Centaur, was now proving himself a source of continual irritation and disgust to the rigidly upright, proud-stepping young Achilles whom he followed. As Rimbaud's poetic ambitions declined, his puritanical bias grew more violent. The slovenliness of Verlaine's spirit, his frivolous self-indulgence, revolted and outraged his friend. Then this was the poetic temperament,—this sly, libidinous, childish being the *sacer vates*, embodiment of the art in which he had hoped to excel! On Rimbaud, the effect of their association was twofold; he was disgusted, disillusioned, but, at the same time, stimulated; by comparison, he felt strong, pure, invincible. "Pitiable brother," he wrote in *Vagabonds*, a prose-poem included in *Les Illuminations*, "what appalling hours of wakefulness I owe him. . . . 'I took advantage of his infirmity. It is through my fault that we shall return home as outcasts and slaves.' For he sup-

posed me at once the irreclaimable harbinger of misfortune and a creature of the strangest innocence. ...
I replied, laughing harshly ... and presently gained
the window, whence across the countryside traversed
by bands of musicians discoursing rare harmonies,
I created the phantoms of future nocturnal splendours." ... Such were *Les Illuminations,* a prophetic
frieze, anticipation of future magnificence, still un-
imagined and unrealized, traversing the intense darkness of his mind. It was Verlaine's function, many
years later, to collect and name them; Rimbaud himself tired of his poems as quickly as he tired of his
friends. His lonely puritanism seems to have excluded friendship; [1] his tenderness was universal:

> Je ne parlerai pas, je ne penserai rien.
> Mais l'amour infini me montera dans l'âme;
> Et j'irai loin, bien loin, comme un bohémien,
> Par la Nature,—heureux comme avec une femme.

Brought face to face with the particular, his asceti-
cism made him distant and hard,—cruel, too. Naturally an adept in the arts of friendship, for all his
instability unswerving and constant, Verlaine became
the *Vierge folle,* foolish, doting virgin, perpetually
wounded but never alienated, whose keenest and
most often recurring fear was lest the belovèd should

[1] Mais l'orgie et la camaraderie des femmes m'étaient interdites. Pas
même un compagnon. Je me voyais devant une foule exaspérée, en face
du peloton d'exécution, pleurant du malheur qu'ils n'aient pu com-
prendre, et pardonnant!—*Une Saison en Enfer.*

desert him: "Je lui faisais promettre qu'il ne me lâcherait pas. Il l'a faite vingt fois, cette promesse d'amant." And, in his character of *Époux infernal*, or Demon Lover, no, he must surely leave him, Rimbaud would reply; it was his duty; . . . "il faudra que je m'en aille, très loin, un jour", meanwhile exploiting this impressionable captive of this charm, this lover whom his "mysterious delicacies" had seduced, who had given up wife and parent for his sake, now lulling him with the serious, unsmiling, womanly softness which he knew how to command, now encouraging him with promises, now transporting him violently to the storm-swept region in which he lived,—from those contacts himself always deriving strength and renewed impetus, in proportion as their recoil upon his friend was weakening and enervating.

Was his renunciation already formulated? In London, Rimbaud had bought one of those high chimney-shaped black hats in which affluence and respectability then walked abroad; the elusive beauty of his features, his pale brilliant eyes, his sullen, mutinously curved mouth, must have been almost completely obliterated by the addition of this sombre covering. It was a symbol which he cherished. Good-bye to beauty as to genius! He had set his mind upon a foothold in the world of men, firmer and more dependable than either genius or beauty could give. His literary exploits, he realized, had been a substitute for the excursions into the world of power, of financial and political eminence, from which youth and poverty had debarred him. He regretted the numerous advantages which might have been and, alas, were not his: "Si j'avais des anté-cédents à un point quelconque de l'histoire de France!—Mais non, rien," he wrote in *Une Saison en Enfer*. And later: "Le sort de fils de famille, cercueil prématuré couvert de limpides larmes. Sans doute la débauche est bête, le vice est bête; il faut jeter la pourriture à l'écart." Is there yet time? he wonders. Other courses of life must, no doubt, be open to him. "L'ennui", he continues, "n'est plus mon amour. Les rages, les débauches, la folie,—dont je sais tous les élans et les désastres,—tout mon fardeau est déposé. Apprécions sans vertige l'étendue de mon innocence." The above sentences, written at a period when he had finally broken away from the old hateful associations and nothing lay betwixt him and the fulfilment of his dream but the impossibility of knowing at exactly what point he would best commence his attack, may, I think,—since resolutions of this sort have usually run through a long heredity before ever they force their way into words, —be read as giving a faithful indication of the much earlier state of mind. It would reveal a lack of courage though, if he did not first regulate his accounts. He must shake off Verlaine; he must compose *Une Saison en Enfer*, setting forth his previous obsessions, depicting the "drôle de ménage" which he had formed with his *Vierge folle* in London and Brussels, expressing his determination henceforward to curtail his appetite that its fare might be the more solid:

> Si j'ai du goût, ce n'est guères
> Que pour la terre et les pierres.
> Je déjeune toujours d'air,
> De roc, de charbons, de fer.

* * *

> Mangez les cailloux qu'on brise,
> Les vielles pierres d'églises;
> Les galets des vieux déluges,
> Pains semés dans les vallées grises.

He does not underestimate the gravity of his new position,—"l'heure nouvelle est au moins très sévère",—nor the degree of failure which it implies: "Moi! moi qui me suis dit mage ou ange, dispensé de toute morale, je suis rendu au sol, avec un devoir à chercher, et la réalité rugueuse à étreindre!" The youngest angel, his imagination was losing its candour; its very excess was ruining him. He was approaching that stage on his journey which, when it is attained, inclines the artist, as he reviews the path by which he has come, to cry out, lamenting the irrecapturable freshness of his youth:

ARTHUR RIMBAUD

O! I cannot, cannot find
The undaunted courage of a virgin mind.

Any virtue, acquired during the journey, shall be put to the test now that he is preparing, absolutely and finally, to rid himself of its benefits. "For I can say that victory is mine: the gnashing of teeth, the hissing of the flames, the poisonous sighs are at length dying down. Abominable memories are growing dimmer. My last regrets are leaving me,—my jealous partiality for beggars, brigands, lovers of death, every sort of backwardness." His new world shall be the world of accepted values, known quantities, substantial rewards. At least, he will be rigorously honest. "Il faut être", he concludes, "absolument moderne."

What remains of Rimbaud's story I need scarcely recapitulate here,—the ruthlessness with which he abandoned and betrayed Verlaine, his rejection of the poet's evangelistic efforts (for he still hated any touch of the spiritual "grossness" which he saw evinced in Verlaine's easy alternation to-and-fro betwixt the blessedness of the saint and the corporeal satisfactions of the sinner)—the obstinate energy that steeled him in his astonishing and unsuccessful battle against the combined forces of circumstance. I have attempted his portrait as a companion and foil to the portrait of Tristan Corbière. No two poets could be more different. *Jemenfoutisme*, as played by its lesser exponents, is a sort of game; because it is a game, it can be sustained indefinitely. The futility of a game lends its professionals a superior, a sometimes inhuman patience. Men tire more quickly where bodies and souls are concerned. The ardour of their embrace, Barbey d'Aurevilly tells us in the story called *Le Bonheur dans le Crime*, is reputed to sterilise the lovers' reproductivity. So immoderate while it endured, Rimbaud's creative fury seems to have killed in his work the reproductive power which exists in the work of many smaller and less generally esteemed writers. His influence is not direct; he has not fertilised directly, as Baudelaire fertilised, and even Jules Laforgue. His influence is widespread; like the dust of a volcanic eruption, it floats along the upper air, drifts gradually through the ether, and will, no doubt, lend our sunsets and our dawns an increased metallic effulgence for yet many years to come. Besides, it has been actually harmful; it has sanctioned innumerable ineptitudes, hoisted innumerable poetasters to an aery elevation from which the subsequent downfall could not be other than painful and ignominious. Rimbaud was a celestial phenomenon, a meteoric sign that, rushing out from among the stars, driving its bolt impetuously into the earth, where it lay blazing and sparkling, made a calcined and uninhabitable zone. Or perhaps we should say that, when Rimbaud threw aside his poetic instrument, he was careful to snap asunder first some essential string. He was emphatic, during his later years, in the disgust with which he regarded his former literary experiments. "Je ne m'occupe plus de ça", he told Delahaye, sadly and contemptuously, in 1879. He was then twenty-four years old; his remark was prohibitive as well as valedictory. It is with a certain hesitation, a certain awkwardness and alarm, that the critic lays his hands upon an instrument which the master-brain who conceived it has broken and incontinently flung away.

*   *   *

Corbière, Rimbaud, Mallarmé,—I have proposed to examine these writers only in so far as their implied differences from one another, and common difference from the poet with whom the foregoing studies have begun, may serve to explain the gradual development or, as you please, deterioration of the always eventful, always restless and relentless human poetic spirit. It is a self-immolatory spirit; it progresses by the constant sacrifice of advantages laboriously and lengthily annexed. Fulke Greville's beautiful quatrain:

> But Love is of the phoenix kind,
> And burnes itselfe, in selfe-made fire,

To breed still new birds in the minde,
From ashes of the old desire . . .

—could be more suitably applied to the cold, cogitative passion which informs great verse.

Million d'oiseaux d'or, ô future Vigueur . . .

—they were unquestionably phoenixes, each awaiting the pyre which should beckon it into existence. Progress, in that sense, we can claim; yet, among those wild, irrational sparklings, we must be very cautious of making arbitrary divisions, of saying *here* an epoch ends; here we cross the threshold; it is a new dispensation we are entering now. . . . Such conclusions must be forced upon us; even so, we must accept them warily. At long intervals, some figure emerges in whose person varying tendencies are summed up. He burns slowly like a censer; he resumes the heterodox opinions, the poetic frailties, the social and intellectual foibles, the refrains and catchwords of his contemporaries, and resolves them to a fine sifted ash. The operation produces that perfume, slightly funereal and slightly hieratic, which his critics are glad to have an opportunity of calling the fragrance of the *fin-de-siècle*. A century is closing it is understood. The poet himself finds the spell of their phrases overpowering. Or a duc des Esseintes is created; the prestige of his imaginary approval is extended over the still-living writer. We have *Prose pour des Esseintes,*—a poem; verses are written for the privilege of his fictitious nod. The censer burns more thickly and more pungently, and a hovering waft of sweetness penetrates and infects the narrow, unfurnished chamber where the muse of a new decade is watching, praying and keeping her hopeful vigil.

In France, institutions are quick to generate; they are positively manufactured, the work of diligent coteries whose potential force towards good, in England,—where processes of this kind do not happen except by inadvertence, a despised and neglected writer thrusting his way into the front rank while his opponents grumble and drowse,—is not generally appreciated. When every Tuesday evening he was at home and young intellectuals, visiting Paris, were as naturally brought to pay him their respects as young *bourgeois* to admire the towers of *Nôtre-Dame* and the *Tour Eiffel*, Mallarmé had become an institution. He supported his functions with great mildness and spirit. Every Tuesday evening Madame Mallarmé and his daughter Geneviève (now Madame Bonniot-Mallarmé) set to work folding back the round table, ranging chairs along the wall, preparing the silk-shaded pendant lamp, putting out a Chinese jar filled with tobacco, providing cigarette-papers and assembling a bouquet of flowers. Then the bell began to ring; Mallarmé opened it himself. A certain simplicity distinguished him, even a kind of serene irony. He would often do his best, Madame Bonnoit-Mallarmé records, to draw his interlocutors into the conversation; they would respectfully demur, and his characteristic monologue, gentle, brilliant, subtly, elaborately inflected, would pursue its usual course. His simplicity and shrewdness he always retained; yet, as his celebrity increased, unwillingly perhaps, or perhaps willingly and amused, his presence was surrounded more and more by various small ritual touches; his modest, elegantly but economically furnished *salon* took on the air of a shrine. Upright beside the white porcelain stove, his chequered shawl captiously arranged across his shoulders, Mallarmé would roll a cigarette.—That was the signal! Firmly and deferentially, the admirer would propound a question, and, quietly extinguishing his match, the Master would glance off upon one of those calculated detours, artfully planned expeditions, in which so unexpectedly placed was the emphasis, so cuningly distributed was the light, that his hearers seemed to traverse a new and exhilarating world—new colours, new forms blooming from amid the ancient amenities of a reverently preserved culture.

No hint of charlatanism betrayed him. Above all, he was sincere, scrupulously honest,—the poet whose art had been learned during a long apprenticeship, under conditions of obscurity and dejection. He was industrious and workman-like; day by day, on little, carefully torn squares of paper, he noted down his linguistic discoveries, storing them with others in a big wooden tea-chest against the moment when they should be embodied in a poem. For when he wrote, it was methodically; he constructed a skeleton, significant words deliberately scattered over his maiden sheet, prearranged schemes of rhyme . . . and within these limits the poem had only to build itself! He was like the magician whom an anthropologist sees, stringing up a row of frail hempen slip-knots, in which he means to snare a favouring wind or entrap the wandering spirits of the dead. So characteristic of his style, the ingenuous single-mindedness with which he went about his ambitious preparations, the extreme elusiveness of the capture he proposed, are also characteristic of the part Mallarmé has played in the formation of modern verse. Does he encourage obliquity? Yet, at the same moment, he advises simplification. He typifies, it would appear, the poet secluded from every outside contact, the poet self-canonised; and yet it was Mallarmé who had declared that the conception of "pure poetry" must entail the virtual abdication of the poet; that the poet must henceforward submit his individual initiative to the initiative of his words,[1]—insinuating, no doubt, that while the rhetorician was

---

[1] L'œuvre pure implique la disparition élocutoire du poète, qui cède l'initiative aux mots.—*Divagations*.

their taskmaster, he, the poet, should be their slave. He would have preferred it, we feel, if his poems could have had a spontaneous generation; he deplored the arrogance of the creator, the creator's bustling inefficiency and noise,—having always at his back the creator's shrilly enunciated desire for "self-expression", and taking refuge from it in a system which should, as far as possible, have excluded the human element, the element of personal hazard, substituting a grave obscurity which is the result of abstruse laws efficiently carried out, where at present there was the chaos of comprehensible observances light-heartedly abused.

He had wished, in fact, to restore to verse those attributes of gravity and repose which Romanticism and Naturalism had so adroitly stolen away. Beyond a certain point, you cannot charge your canvas with "expression"; there comes a moment at which the saint's glassy orb cannot roll more glassily, when the Madonna's beatific smile, dawning gradually through the centuries, from a pucker scarcely perceptible at the corners of the lips to the gaping rictus, imposed by Italian seventeenth-century taste, cannot be further enlarged. Then a poet thinks regretfully of the beauty of inanimate and inexpressive things,—of Rome, depopulated by the Barbarian invasions, till the statues outnumbered the men;—of statues themselves, their precise oblongs of shade, statues isolated upon the summits of lofty buildings, their features almost unrecognizable, their eyes worn lidless by the rain and frost, their icy gestures of defiance, command, benediction, sailing magnificently against a stormy sky or settling down into the twilight among a cloud of birds. Unlike the poets of Romanticism, he will appreciate in the statue, not its similarity to humankind, but, on the contrary, its strangeness. Taken prisoner, he may reflect, by men, compelled to serve as material for their horrible ingenuity (their ineradicable itch,—of something to make something else!), this stone, under its convict-dress, *hero, archangel* or *emperor*, still preserves the native integrity of the block. Stonily, it infers the unquarried defiance of the inanimate. Thus, Mallarmé's world, and the more recent world of his successor and disciple, M. Paul Valéry, is a world in which silence and immobility have recovered their original sway; the narrow rivulet of verse is designed to accentuate the unwritten potentialities of the margin. After the tyranny of poets by whom every *tic* had been dignified under the name of gesture, every convulsive grimace had been considered the index of a profound and noteworthy emotion, a poet can find the calm he requires only in the voiceless and expressionless region of geometric shapes:

> De nos lits de cristal
> Nous fûmes éveillées,

Des griffes de métal
Nous ont appareillées.

*   *

Servantes sans genoux,
Sourires sans figures,
La belle devant nous
Se sent les jambes pures,

Pieusement pareilles,
Le nez sous le bandeau
Et nos riches oreilles
Sourdes au blanc fardeau . . .

—runs M. Valéry's *Cantique des Colonnes*. Similarly,
as he becomes accustomed to the world of images
Mallarmé has created, a sort of sculptural rigidity
strikes the reader's eye. The poet, whose life,
patiently composed from the most unpromising sub-
stances, had resembled a *nature morte*,—his domestic
happiness, his harmonious and peaceful interior, his
animals and flowers, his books, his correspondence,
—also carried into the life of the imagination the
same affectionate regard for minute particulars, the
same preference for emotional tranquillity maintained in equilibrium by constant intellectual stress,
which had kept free his personal life from any
tumults except, of course, those which are brain-
born. His verse will recall sometimes the unearthly
precision of a sick-room or bed-ridden paralytic's
chamber; there is whiteness, space, a single flower

blooming self-consciously in its glass, the presence of a few carefully chosen and eminently sympathetic friends, the rare but insubstantial fruits, blossoms and sweetmeats that they have brought. . . . Here even the mirror suggests an expanse of frozen water:

> O miroir!
> Eau froide par l'ennui dans ton cadre gelée
> Que de fois, et pendant les heures, désolée
> Des songes et cherchant mes souvenirs qui sont
> Comme des feuilles sous ta glace au trou profond,
> Je m'apparus en toi comme une ombre lointaine . . .

—the frozen pool a swan who had once furrowed its surface, this swan a poet; till, finally, we have become inured to the sort of crystalline exasperation which gave Mallarmé's poems, and has given the poems of M. Paul Valéry, not only their fineness and their hardness, their exquisite impersonal chill, but, incidentally, that air of sustained protest,—the air as of one continually lamenting "flights unflown", poetic impulses frozen on the wing,—which pervades the first eight lines of Mallarmé's beautiful sonnet:

> Le vierge, le vivace et le bel aujourd'hui
> Va-t-il nous déchirer avec un coup d'aile ivre
> Ce lac dur oublié que hante sous le givre
> Le transparent glacier des vols qui n'ont pas fui!
>
> Un cygne d'autrefois se souvient que c'est lui
> Magnifique mais qui sans espoir se délivre

STÉPHANE MALLARMÉ

Pour n'avoir pas chanté la région où vivre
Quand du stérile hiver a resplendi l'ennui.

Like leaves imprisoned beneath thick ice, which
the poet mentions in a passage I have transcribed
above, Mallarmé's *concetti*, his *Petits Vers*, inscrip-
tions for fans, enigmatic and melodious stanzas to
be copied into the pages of an album, verse epistles,
rhyming envelopes, are less fluttering and ephemeral
than from the nature of such productions we usually
expect. Imagine a clear sheet of ice, solid, unflawed,
allowing the passer-by to look down and examine
its depths, the ingenuous aspirations which lay im-
mobilised there, the combed-out tresses of the stream,
drowned refuse and all the wrack and wastage of
circumstance. . . . Yet under this translucent covering, to-and-fro moves an inconstant, small brilliant
flame, glowing through its coffin-lid, momentarily
transforming the icy, motionless fronds among which
it is immured. "Il détient le génie, la puissance, la
gloire," Mallarmé said, after visiting Victor Hugo,
"mais il lui manque une petite flamme que j'ai et que
je voudrais lui donner." The consciousness of genius,
Mallarmé's preoccupation with the Word, its lofty
obsession,—"donner un sens plus pur aux mots de
la tribu",—so irradiates his verse that although,
during his search for a poetic formula which should
have enabled him to put his hands on the essential
part of every poet's inspiration—(the long-drawn

melancholy cadence of Baudelaire's autumnal dirge,
what critics have called his *miaulement* or voluptuous
feline wail)—he seems to have destroyed the sententious magniloquence of the ancient poetry by ex-
cluding its rhetorical basis, equally he would seem
to have re-endowed it with that interior dispassionate glow which, if it had not altogether lost, it was
then in some great danger of losing. Convinced that
literary expression had grown too elastic, that its
channels were too accommodating, the writer was
concerned to erect fresh obstacles, since we can best
achieve solitude by retreating on to a plane where the
larger number of our contemporaries will not care
to follow. Yet it was no mere immunity from latter-
day contacts that Mallarmé sought; the sympathies
which actuated him had little or nothing in common
with that cultivated depravation of literary taste,
summed up in the protagonist of Huysmans' lugu-
brious romance. Mallarmé, we should remember,
was a student of English verse; he had learned to
appreciate the magical *immediacy* of effect which is
the occasional, precarious and hard-won privilege
of certain English writers. After a thousand beauties,
so many of them cumulative, which the fulness of
time brings into being, which their context gradually
matures, the sudden emergence of some felicitous
image, springing like a group of sea-gods where a
moment earlier there was vacancy, flowering like a

wave where we could distinguish only the bare, uneventful swelling and subsiding movement of the verse, is startling and peculiarly delightful to a foreign ear:

> He . . .
> . . . question'd every gust of rugged wings
> That blows from off each beaked Promontory,
> They knew not of his story
> And sage Hippotades their answer brings,
> That not a blast was from his dungeon stray'd,
> *The air was calm and on the level brine*
> *Sleek Panope and all her sisters play'd.*

Then the doctrine of "pure poetry" is the invention of a poet, whom sophistication has taught to recognise the immediate quality of great verse, whom sophistication has also debarred from that intimate and unflinching acquaintance with the commonplace by which, in the past, poetic sublimity has so often been accompanied and favoured. Laforgue's criticism of Baudelaire, written perhaps fifteen years after his master's death, is already eloquent of a change; retrospectively, he admires the elder poet's hardihood, "his manner of saying,—and that without any expense of prudish parenthesis but perfectly plain and to the point,—the familiarity of some great martyr which emboldens him to say:

> Les persiennes abris des secrètes luxures

and on the next page:

> Andromaque, je pense à vous!

—adding (so humanly) 'veuve d'Hector, hélas'. This 'hélas' is neither Racinien commonplace nor yet is it a device to fill up the line, but a moving and great-hearted subtlety." . . .

Laforgue's enthusiastic sentences already sound a valedictory note; the critic himself had already abandoned his youthful Baudelairean imitations. Mallarmé, in his turn, had emulated Baudelaire's directness:

> Mais, hélas! Ici-bas est maître: sa hantise
> Vient m'écœurer parfois jusqu'en cet abri sûr,
> Et le vomissement impur de la Bêtise
> Me force à me boucher le nez devant l'azur.
>
> Est-il moyen, ô Moi qui connais l'amertume,
> D'enfoncer le cristal par le monstre insulté
> Et de m'enfuir, avec mes deux ailes sans plume
> — Au risque de tomber pendant l'éternité?

These essays, *Les Fenêtres* and other poems, though they are not the least admirable part of his achievement, Mallarmé had superseded. Art, he knew, treads instinctively a circular road; it is only by a resolute attention to the future that a poet can come abreast again with the irrecapturable graces of the past.

But Mallarmé's poetic dogma, his subsequent practice of it, the partial yet still not unmagnificent failure to which it so nearly led him, must remain definitely outside the scope of my present brief survey. In the study of a poet's derivations, his theory will often seem to have left smaller trace upon the minds of his literary successors than, perhaps, some trick he may have had of slightly disarranging the natural order of his sentences, some frequently recurring choice of imagery, odd inflection or individual manner of broaching his subject. For are not these the manifestations of that "acquired difficulty" with which, Joubert said, it was important that our inborn facility should be overlaid? A poet's dogma, comparatively, is factitious, our appetite for it manufactured. From Mallarmé we have derived, not so much the dogmatic trend of his weekly *causeries*, their matter, as the accomplished and persuasive manner in which they were delivered. The shrewd simplicity with which Mallarmé set off upon his most difficult flights,—modern writers, each according to the degree of his individual weakness, have inherited *that*; they have inherited alike his love of detour and his hatred of prefatory rhetoric:

"Nul, que je me rappelle" (he wrote, introducing his short *Souvenir* of Villiers de l'Isle-Adam) "ne fut, par un vent d'illusion, engouffré dans les plis visibles tombant de son geste ouvert qui signifiait: 'Me voici', avec une impulsion aussi véhémente et surnaturelle, poussé, que jadis cet adolescent" . . . —a passage it would be almost impossible to translate, but which, both in its elaboration and in its abruptness is extraordinarily reminiscent of the modern prose method. "Me voici", exclaims the modern writer, none the less shaking out between us the folds of his mysterious *pudeur*. It was Mallarmé, was it not, who taught him this air of proffering a solution when he wishes to propound an enigma;— from Mallarmé, among others, that he learned this deceptive air of extra-lucidity, this ambiguous clarity of his which is so much more impenetrable than any attempt at deliberate mystification;—Mallarmé who, before ever M. Jean Cocteau put it into words, formulated the principle of tact in audacity?—"Le tact dans l'audace c'est de savoir *jusqu'où on peut aller trop loin.*"

Tact, deliberation, *finesse*—it is not in the revolt from tradition that the spirit of modern literature is comprised, but in a regard for tradition so intense that it inspires the modern artist with a certain embarrassment, a certain creative *gêne*. Our sense of the historical quality of the present, the topical quality of the past, past and present, so to speak, interleaved and the "message" they contain only read as one,— these apprehensions, though they have fathered the little we can show of concrete aesthetic achievement, M. Valéry's poems, the draughtsmanship of Picasso, the statuary of Maillol, have produced their corresponding defects. We are grown more timid than our predecessors; our audacities are shorter lived. M. Jean Cocteau himself,—and M. Cocteau is a brilliant novelist, a sensitive if unstable liaison-officer, connecting the different arts,—after proclaiming his *Rappel à l'ordre*, a courageous return towards simplicity, has also demonstrated to what ingenious and trifling effect that "return" can be exploited. He proves as witty and as versatile as Mallarmé on the editorial staff of *La Dernière Mode*. The modern painter has discovered fresh outlets for his pictorial sentiment, the modern novelist for his sentimental bias. New heresies are abroad. "Amusing" has become a word which offers immense possibilities of evasion.

*   *   *

Critics, whose temperament places them under the necessity of writing epitaphs, may conclude that, in the truest sense of the phrase, our own period is the twilight of literature, previous generations insensibly declining towards it, and that, when dusk has at last fallen upon the products of our Silver Age, the dispassionate scrutiny of the moon will reveal them for what they are,—dead things, perfectly cold and stark. Yet, since the critic has usually a deeper grudge against the World, dimly personified, than ever he nurses against Literature,—Edenic region, peopled by happy individuals who have avoided this ineluctable penance, of being a professional critic,—he may add a rider, expressing his sympathy with the defunct and giving it as his opinion that, though the course which Literature has recently pursued was, it seems to him, frankly suicidal, still, more blame attaches to a world which, instead of sustaining and encouraging, did literally press it out of life; the artist is less reprehensible than his patron. . . . But here I should like to suggest that the gradual process of abdication with which the foregoing studies, all of them, at one point or another deal, was, in fact, a voluntary gesture. Nor can we admit the critic's artificial symmetry of nicely apportioned praise and blame. The poetic spirit has its secret channels and inlets, currents and tides and tempests, worthy of the destructive and unpredictable whimsicalities of the ocean itself. To-day it runs backward and, deserting the granite quays of the river-front, the palace steps, temple-stairs built for sacred lustrations and the many and heavy-laden vessels of rhetoric which it used to carry, seeks the pleasantly meandering, sedgy channels which lie nearer its source. Something, perhaps, of a Merovingian age our period is, our artists resembling those long-haired Merovingian potentates who refused the cumbrous paraphernalia of their sovereignty and, as against the pleasures of a palace and a kingdom, were philosophic enough to prefer their few fields and garden and the smoky shelter of a farmhouse roof. For we have seen the painter, abandoning the dearly bought apparatus of an elaborate technique, consent to learn afresh in the school of artists who, coming to their art most of them without prepossessions or any sort of professional training, had envisaged its problem from a new and illuminating angle. Beauty is the rarebird which, recognizing the fowler's tread, can still be snared now and again by the hand that feigns a generous ineptitude, which flings downs its nets carelessly and inconsequently. . . . Even the canons of modern elegance,—simply-cut dresses insisting on the absence of ornament, sparsely-furnished rooms emphasizing their cubic content of empty unimpeded space, squarely-cut jewelry, leanly-designed vehicles,—are expressive of a generation more cautious than daring, which, since we appreciate every investment in proportion as it is quickly realized, recoils horror-struck before the extravagant commitments of our Romantic predecessors.

Ages less "enlightened" have predicted the approaching conflagration of the universe and, whole communities together, their lamps ready and loins girded up, have lived in the perpetual expectation of a fiery or sanguinary end. Then the precious stone, which could be knotted into the corner of a handkerchief, became more desirable than lands and houses; and similarly, while I must not go so far as to suggest that an atmosphere of apocalyptic dread has pervaded the entire fabric of modern civilization, we

notice a contemporary preference for those forms of
art Jules Laforgue had prophesied when he spoke of
"l'Art sans poitrine", slender, bosomless Art,—Art
compact and imponderable, as though, during our
flight from some new inroad of the Barbarians, we
anticipated having to carry away our goddess precariously slung across our shoulders. Then, the ex-
plosions of creative energy are limited, no tremen-
dous frescoes painted; no heroic and didactic poems
are written. Architecture, an art formerly devoted to
the magnanimous celebration of man's supremacy
over nature, crushing down the tender waves of the
earth with its accumulation of churches and palaces,
must take on a new kind of grace, rigid, dehuman-
ised, mechanical; it must serve utility now, assimilate
the battleship's line, the spacious efficiency of the
workshop. Le Corbusier's city is Laputa only lacking the power of locomotion. These houses are not
rooted in the earth; they are miniature flying palaces;
each of them is a railway carriage immobilized. They
would accommodate a people of exiles, a race whose
spiritual exile was already an accomplished fact,
whose territorial expulsion had already almost begun,
who were retiring steadily, in good order, the scenes
of whose one-time magnificence were rushing past
the windows, their political foibles, their successive
literary moods,—Romanticism, Naturalism and, last
of all, Symbolism.